Getting Going in Europe

Richard Armitage is a project development specialist whose interests include accessible passenger transport, local economic development, clean technologies, publishing and journalism. He was the Community Transport Association's founding General Secretary (1984–90) and currently acts as technical adviser to the *Buses for All – Europe* campaign. He writes regularly in a range of professional journals.

Richard Macfarlane is an independent researcher and consultant, specialising in local economic development and voluntary sector management in Britain and Europe. He has been a member of pan-European research teams and has experienced at first hand many of the problems described in this book.

NCVO – voice of the voluntary sector

NCVO champions the cause of the voluntary sector and works to improve its effectiveness, identify unmet needs and encourage initiatives to meet them.

Established in 1919 as the representative body for the voluntary sector in England, NCVO now gives voice to some 600 national organisations – from large 'household name' charities to small self-help groups involved in all areas of voluntary and social action. It is also in touch with thousands of other voluntary bodies and groups, and has close links with government departments, local authorities, institutions of the European Union and the business sector.

About the Directory of Social Change

DSC is a registered educational charity, based in London and Liverpool, which aims to promote the more effective use of charitable resources. As well as publishing guides and handbooks, it runs training courses and conferences on fundraising, financial management, communications and other charity issues. DSC is also the organiser of Charityfair, the annual national exhibition and showcase for charities.

Getting Going in Europe

A Guide to Developing Transnational Projects

Richard Armitage and
Richard Macfarlane

 NCVO Publications

Published in association with
DIRECTORY OF SOCIAL CHANGE

Published by
NCVO Publications
(incorporating Bedford Square Press)
imprint of the
National Council for Voluntary
Organisations
Regent's Wharf, 8 All Saints Street,
London N1 9RL and
Directory of Social Change
Radius Works, Back Lane,
London NW3 1HL

First published 1994

Typeset by Linda Parker
Printed in Great Britain by Page Bros.,
Norwich

A catalogue record for this book is
available from the British Library.

ISBN 0 7199 1397 7

Contents

Foreword

This book is for all voluntary sector organisations to encourage them to get going in Europe. It contains something of interest for people working at different levels within the sector:

- policy and strategy: directors or co-ordinators of smaller national voluntary organisations, of larger regional voluntary organisations, and of the largest local ones;
- development and project work: development or project managers, or people with responsibility for Europe, in larger voluntary organisations;
- fundraising: organisations that are pursuing European funding and therefore need to establish partnership arrangements with counterparts in other member states.

In the latter category, the book will also be of interest to local authorities, TECs, and other public bodies that are seeking funding based on partnerships in Europe.

The book offers practical ideas and suggestions to help people 'get off the mark'. It provides an overview of what is involved, and uses case studies to demonstrate other organisations' experience of action at a European level.

Much of the information set out here was derived from a series of three workshops organised by the National Council for Voluntary Organisations and the Directory of Social Change in 1993. These brought together practitioners from a range of community and voluntary organisations already working in Europe, and a mixed group of voluntary sector workers who were keen to learn from this experience. In addition, we asked some experienced individuals to highlight key aspects of good practice in a short postal questionnaire, and a number of case studies have been prepared.

Thanks must go to all those who participated in the workshops and who facilitated the case studies. Without them it would not have been possible to produce this review of good practice.

Richard Armitage
Richard Macfarlane
June 1994

Glossary

In any technical document, it is necessary to use shorthand, in order to avoid long sentences and repetition. A new set of institutions and political arrangements has been created in Europe since the end of the Second World War, and with it has come a large number of new names, acronyms, abbreviations and expressions. The following list is intended to make reading the book easier.

CDA   A co-operative development agency (UK)

CDF   Community Development Foundation
A UK charity promoting community development

CIS   Commonwealth of Independent States (formerly USSR)

CKH   Charity Know How
A UK grants fund set up jointly by the Foreign Office and leading grant-making trusts to fund know-how exchanges between Britain and Eastern Europe

CVS   Council for Voluntary Service (UK)
A network of local agencies which support and service their local voluntary sector

DG   Directorate-General of the European Commission
The Commission bureaucracy is handled by departments called directorates-general; each one has a director-general who reports to at least one commissioner. Each DG is numbered (usually with a roman numeral)

DGXI   Environment Directorate-General

EC   European Commission
The executive arm of the European Union, based in Brussels,

which initiates common policies, introduces legislation, and administers EU funds

ECAS   Euro-Citizen-Action-Service
A Brussels-based advocacy and information service whose objective is to strengthen the voice of voluntary sector associations within the EU; the citizen's watchdog, aiming to create a better balance between public interest and corporate lobbying

EIC   European Information Centre
A network of EC-financed centres spread throughout the EU

ESF   European Social Fund
Fund set up under the Treaty of Rome to promote employment opportunities and geographical and occupational mobility for workers within the EU

EU   European Union
Until 1994, known as the European Community; the Union comprises 12 member states, due to be increased to 16 with the accession of Austria, Finland, Norway and Sweden

ICOM   Industrial Common Ownership Movement
A UK national organisation promoting and servicing worker and other co-operative enterprises

NCVO   National Council for Voluntary Organisations
The national body involved in policy analysis and formation for the English voluntary sector; there are equivalent bodies in Northern Ireland, Scotland and Wales

NGO   Non-governmental organisation

TEC   Training and Enterprise Council (UK)

UFJT   Union de Foyers pour les Jeunes Travailleurs
The French Foyer federation, which is developing the Foyer concept for young homeless people across Europe

sector   An area of work for voluntary organisations (such as the youth sector, older people, refugees and so on); hence multi-sectoral, meaning 'covers several sectors'

1 Introduction

This book is based on the premise that the UK voluntary sector cannot remain aloof from the major alterations made to the political map of Europe in recent years. The tearing down of the Berlin Wall was only one – albeit highly visible – symbol of the magnitude of these changes. Whilst old, familiar concerns undoubtedly remain, there is a growing realisation that they can no longer be tackled in the same ways as before. Poverty, for example, manifests itself as always in terms of individual misery and despair, yet more and more there is a European dimension to anti-poverty strategies.

Organisations which have already become involved in activity on a European scale are discovering comfortable assumptions about spheres of influence and levels of operation are constantly challenged:

- If resources are limited, is it better to spend time and effort in London or Brussels?
- Will links with local community development projects across Europe provide greater mutual support than membership of the local CVS?
- Can we operate at all the old levels – local, regional, national, sectoral – and at a European level too?
- Are some of the existing lines of communication becoming superfluous, standing in the way of fresh developments?

1.1 Partnerships and projects in Europe

The last decade has seen a rapid increase in the number of UK community and voluntary organisations that include a European element in their work. There are three specific reasons for this:

- the wish of the EC to foster closer working relationships between the peoples of the EU member states. To encourage this they have introduced

1

funding regimes that require parallel applications from organisations in more than one member state, which are committed to working together if their bids are successful.

• the collapse of communism in Eastern Europe and the need to replace the state-managed economic and social welfare systems. This has created a demand for information about 'the West European way' and opportunities for transmitting ideas and 'good practice' from the UK community and voluntary sectors.

• the desire by UK campaigns to use European legal and political institutions as another means of achieving change, especially when they feel little progress is likely at national level in the UK, or where competence for the issue has shifted to Brussels.

For many UK voluntary and community organisations the initial contact with Europe is the EC, through fundraising and lobbying activities. Good practice in undertaking these operations has been adequately presented in other publications (see Chapter 12) and will not be dealt with here. Our focus in this book is the establishment of partnerships and projects for the delivery of services or the advancement of a cause. There are three levels of involvement:

• where community and voluntary organisations from several European countries share information, ideas and experience;

• where parallel projects are developed and run in the same service area or sector, but in different European countries;

• where a UK organisation sets up a branch or an operational partnership in a European country, or of a non-UK organisation in the UK.

1.2   Time to act

With so much change happening so swiftly, and with nation states and European institutions working to agendas over which the UK voluntary sector has had virtually no influence, it is unsurprising that many voluntary organisations are increasingly worried that they may be missing out. This book will help you get started. It is intended to be reassuring, without being complacent. The UK voluntary sector as a whole is already making its mark on the European stage, and, by and large, the consensus of those who are involved is that the effort is worth while. But whilst it is not too late to 'get going in Europe', it *is* the right moment to be making a thorough assessment of the extent to which action at a European level should form part of your organisation's portfolio of work.

2 Europe Beckons

2.1 Going abroad

For some UK-based voluntary organisations there is a simple motivation for getting involved in Europe: one part of their 'mission' is to 'export' the service that has initially been developed in Britain to other countries. If the service has been successful in the UK in tackling problems which are known to exist in other countries, then it follows that people who are dedicated to taking action on these issues may seek to do so on an international basis. Charity may begin at home, but it certainly need not stay at home.

The international organisation promotes the formation of national organisations in all parts of the world and helps them evaluate their services. In the absence of a national organisation Befrienders International enables new centres to develop and provides a central resource for management training and fundraising material. *(from promotional material of Befrienders International, the international arm of The Samaritans)*

Corporate community involvement is a robust idea, capable of leading to benefits wherever the market economy operates. It had developed on its own primarily in the UK and US and the view was taken that, with a coherent presentation and a committed organisation, useful work could also take place in other countries – including European ones. *(James Jolly, The Prince of Wales Business Leaders Forum)*

So, for one range of organisations, working in Europe is not an option: it is a necessity. In these organisations there may be some commitment to exchanging ideas, but this may be less important than promoting the ideals and experience of the UK-based body. For example, there is a wide range of organisations which provide assistance to people who are potential suicides, but members of Befrienders International are expected to subscribe to a set of principles and a set of practices which together represent the philosophy of 'befriending'.

For others, working in Europe is important because the issue they are dealing with has a multinational dimension – whether immigration and migrant communities, the environment or wildlife preservation (birds as well as pollution cross national borders), or poverty and exclusion (as unemployment in Europe is a Europe-wide problem). For others again, going abroad stems from a desire to share expertise and help solve problems elsewhere (for example, setting up voluntary services in Eastern Europe). And for yet others, internationalism is at the very heart of how they wish to operate (for example, the Waldorf and Steiner schools).

2.2   Progress through exchange

For another set of community and voluntary organisations involved in Europe there is less commitment to their existing philosophy and practices: they are looking for European projects with which they can exchange ideas and experience as a means of mutual learning.

> East Anglian Co-operative Development Agency has been actively seeking to develop good trans-national partnerships . . . for work study exchanges for co-operatives and their support organisations. *(Rachel Sleet, Co-ordinator, East Anglian CDA)*

For some, the primary aim is to 'import' ideas and experience from other European countries. For example, the Foyer Federation for Youth is seeking to develop young people's accommodation, training and employment projects in the UK, based on a long-established French system. They got involved in Europe because the French Foyer federation (UFJT) was keen to spread the concept across Europe:

> The French have visited the UK probably twenty times over the last two years to talk to anyone who is interested in the Foyer concept. *(Don Macdonald, Secretary, Foyer Federation for Youth).*

A European Network of Foyers was formed with UK representation from Shelter. They spread information about the work within the UK, and the Foyer Federation was formed. The benefits of this approach are the opportunity to learn from the experience of others and start to see things from a different, perhaps less parochial, point of view, and the chance to spark off brand new ideas (for solving old problems) or even begin to identify new issues and original approaches.

2.3 Networks

Whilst this book is not primarily concerned with lobbying, it is important to recognise that involvement in Europe-wide networks, and joint action with projects from other countries, can enhance an organisation's ability to influence the policy of European institutions (such as the European Commission and the European Parliament). Unless you join together with similar bodies from other member states or work through European networks, it is difficult to get your point of view heard at the European level and you become largely limited to lobbying nationally. Such influence is important in creating a context within which UK and other European projects are able to achieve their objectives, especially with regard to the formation of legislation (an increasing amount of regulation now derives from Brussels) and the allocation of EC budgets.

> This report will not list in detail the major policy or micro-economic and social changes that have occurred within Europe in 1992. Clearly the moves towards the single market and the post Maastricht summit debates are central, and linked to this the serious stresses facing communities in Eastern Europe with the related factors of migration and ethnic conflict.
>
> As a UK-based agency, CDF has been concerned to understand and mobilise the community sector's influence upon these changes, as they affect Britain's regions and localities, and to promote the community development perspective within European policy.
>
> In operationalising our work we have adopted a partnership approach, as well as taking the lead on individual initiatives. Our chief 'joint venture' partners during this year across Europe have been the member agencies of the Combined European Bureau for Social Development. *(Community Development Foundation European Annual Report 1992)*

> I visited Humagora, a French version of the UK Charity Fair, in April 1994. I was struck by the wide range of French voluntary organisations concerned with poverty and exclusion. I'm sure we have a lot to learn and share on what is essentially now a pan-European problem. I am now in discussion with the organisers of Humagora on the idea of a European event designed to share ideas on action against poverty. *(Michael Norton, Director, Directory of Social Change)*

2.4 Seeking finance

The search for EC funding has drawn a significant number of UK community and voluntary organisations into Europe. In recent years, the EC has made it a condition of funding that applicants find partner organisations which are undertaking similar tasks in other member states, or which are part of a multinational project. In the former situation the project applying for funds has to locate and develop a relationship with at least one partner organisation. In the latter, they must agree to participate in international programme activities, such as visiting other projects, attending training sessions and exchanging information.

However, it seems that where these 'forced partnerships' are stimulating and useful, voluntary organisations will seek to continue them long after the first joint project finished.

East Anglian CDA got involved in European Social Fund trans-national programmes in 1988 when its first applications to the ESF for funding training programmes for the long-term unemployed were accepted. Under the terms (then in operation) projects in East Anglia and the South East which were aimed at the long-term unemployed would not succeed in attracting ESF matched funding unless they were trans-national in their scope. This meant that in order to get ESF funding we had to find European partners. *(Rachel Sleet, East Anglian CDA)*

In a number of policy areas the EC is considered to be more sympathetic than the UK government to what local people are seeking to fund. This attracts many community and voluntary organisations to explore EC funding and clearly the requirement of a partnership approach encourages increasing contact between UK projects and similar bodies in Europe.

There is also the possibility of putting together a consortium bid through a lead agency, which might be a larger voluntary organisation or a local authority. For example, Camden Community Transport, which provides a wide range of local passenger transport services, was a partner with the London Borough of Camden and several private sector companies in a £2 million bid submitted to the EC LIFE programme in March 1994. Putting this proposal together required the preparation of a detailed technical and financial submission, and discussions and negotiations with the participating firms, against a very tight deadline.

A by-product of the rather complex application procedures for EC funds is that the staff of UK projects obtain new experience of fundraising. This is a skill which they can apply in other areas.

2.5 Personal goals and individual commitment

A common feature of most community and voluntary organisations is the high level of personal commitment by their staff and volunteers to the organisation's aims and objectives. It is therefore not surprising that these individuals should want to tackle similar problems in other parts of the world.

It is not unusual for organisations to get involved in Europe because senior workers or management committee members 'want to do something' and feel that the UK organisation has something to offer.

> Active in Eastern Europe since its inception in 1990 as a personal initiative of The Prince of Wales, the Business Leaders Forum promotes the view that business interests are best served if business shows itself ready and able to become involved in improving the communities in which it seeks to operate and thrive. *(from* Meeting The Challenge, *The Prince of Wales Business Leaders Forum)*

In other cases individuals who have a personal commitment may initiate a project in Europe and then obtain the support of an organisation for their work.

> My Latin teacher introduced me to Russian literature when I was 16 and I became hooked on Russia and the Russians. After twenty years I was invited, in 1988, to take a school group on an official exchange and to receive the first group of school children allowed out of the Soviet Union. School exchanges have taken place every year since then.
>
> At the same time close links were being established between Exeter and Yaroslavl, where my family and I have many friends; my daughter studies at Yaroslavl University and my husband is now teaching there temporarily.
>
> Soon after my mother had died in a hospice, virtually without pain and with all possible support from a dedicated team, one of the grannies I used to visit in Moscow died in appalling circumstances. I investigated the care of the dying in Russia and decided to try and establish a hospice in our twin city. I have had talks with senior medical administrators and doctors in Yaroslavl; and with Charity Know How money I have been able to invite some of them to Exeter to see hospice care for themselves. *(Patricia Cockerell, Exeter)*

East–West Link was established in 1992 under the management of Charity Know How Fund to encourage and facilitate working relationships between UK organisations and their East European counterparts, so that they could share experiences and offer technical support. It was interesting when setting up this initiative to discover how much similar activity was already taking place on an informal basis. For example, the Director of the National Extension College was advising an organisation in Bulgaria on developing distance learning, and the Director of Centrepoint had been asked for advice by a Russian organisation dealing with young homeless people.

2.6   Staff development

Getting involved in Europe offers fresh challenges and opportunities for staff development. This can be useful in two situations:

- where budget cuts in the UK are limiting the growth of voluntary and community organisations and it is difficult to provide opportunities for personal growth and advancement within the organisation, extending the organisation's work in Europe represents a growth opportunity for both the organisation and its existing staff;
- where staff have been successfully delivering a service for a period of time and it may become difficult for them to maintain the same high level of motivation and commitment, European work can provide an exciting stimulus.

2.7   Broadening our horizons

The above review suggests that, for many organisations, getting involved in Europe serves a function for the organisation and its staff. However, for some organisations the aims and the outputs are more nebulous but no less significant.

Going to see how people in other countries tackle common problems can lead to a reassessment of the UK organisation's assumptions. Learning from others can cover a much wider range of activities than just project delivery.

Taking volunteers and users from the UK to meet local people involved in similar work in Europe can help them put their own experience in perspective. They can see that their problems are not purely local, and maybe they will appreciate just how well they are doing in solving them. Alternatively, they will see others' solutions, offering them fresh hope and energy when they return home.

Attending conferences is one way of finding out more. The Volonteurope conference on volunteer management or the International Fundraising Workshop, both held annually in the Netherlands, bring together practitioners from across Europe and further afield. Whilst you are there, you can also make your own contacts and links simply by asking what are the most interesting projects (in your field) and then arranging to visit them.

In 1993, as part of its programme for the European Year of Older People and Solidarity Between Generations, the Transport Resource Unit of Greater Manchester CVS organised two study tours to Utrecht and Cologne, and to Barcelona. Altogether 20 people travelled, including 16 older people. The aim was to compare aspects of public transport provision in the different cities with that of Greater Manchester.

On balance, the groups felt that the concessionary fare scheme which operates in Greater Manchester compares fairly well with the experience in Germany, Netherlands and Spain . . .

. . . Utrecht provided the group with an example of a complex and comprehensive transport interchange, linked also to extensive shopping facilities. Rail, bus and the Sneltram all operate out of the central station and the important place which public transport had in serving the city is clearly evident. The smooth operation showed up the congestion and the lack of co-ordination which marks bus operations around Piccadilly Gardens in central Manchester.

. . . Since returning from their tours, the participants have already had a number of opportunities to relate their experiences to others who belong to the same clubs and organisations (such as Age Concern Thameside, Stockport Probus, Manchester's College of the Third Age, and the retired members union branches of the TGWU and RMT). *(from* Using Public Transport: Comparing notes from older people travelling in the European Union, *GMCVS Transport Resource Unit, 1993)*

The interaction of local people from different countries helps to spread the idea of 'one world': it helps to replace suspicion with understanding. Furthermore, where people are not experienced travellers and are giving their time on a voluntary basis, there is a much greater appreciation of the reality that getting involved with the people of Europe can be fun!

3 *Working in Other European Countries*

Many organisations based in the UK have begun to work in other European countries. The experience of two of them is described below.

3.1 Befrienders International – extending into Eastern Europe

Befrienders International (BI) was established in 1974 as the international 'umbrella' body of the Samaritan movement. Over 300 befriending centres are operating in 30 countries. Although the largest number are in the UK and the Republic of Ireland, about one-third are elsewhere, with a particular concentration in Brazil.

There are many crisis centres and helplines operating across many countries. Those which become members of BI are committed to 'seven principles and seven practices' that determine the range of services to be offered, and the manner in which they are delivered. Key elements are:

- a service based on listening and supporting, rather than advising or instructing
- confidentiality and the right of the caller to break contact at any time
- the use of volunteers who are carefully selected, trained and supported
- a service that is not influenced by any political, philosophical or religious beliefs

The role of BI is to encourage the formation of associations that subscribe to its principles and practices, and (where no national network exists) to enable new centres to be established through the provision of advice and training on management, fundraising and service delivery. This implies a belief in the particular set of operating principles developed by The Samaritans in the UK, the Republic of Ireland, and BI more widely.

The democratisation process in Eastern Europe has resulted in opportunities for greater contact with existing crisis and helpline services, and people who are interested in establishing more services. It is within BI's terms of reference to nurture these contacts. This has been done through visits: experienced volunteers from UK centres have gone to Hungary, Poland and the CIS, and volunteers from local projects have been to the UK. While the explicit aim of these visits is often to run or attend workshops on BI principles and operating practices, the visits have fulfilled some wider functions:

- introducing novel issues for local projects, for example, the explicit discussion of suicidal feelings with callers, a topic previously avoided;
- undertaking promotional work for struggling projects:
    - by stimulating a media discussion of the 'crisis services',
    - giving credibility by showing the links with international practice,
    - and by meeting state officials;
- generally raising the levels of knowledge about the provision of crisis services in other countries and encouraging an examination of local practices.

Membership of an international organisation such as BI helps reduce the sense of isolation felt by these centres. Increasingly, the centres are providing their own mutual support and co-operation through correspondence and joint training workshops. The twinning of centres in Eastern Europe and the former Soviet Union with Samaritan branches in the UK and the Republic of Ireland also plays a crucial role in the exchange of information and the sharing of ideals.

However, the BI experience of working in Eastern Europe has raised a number of issues that must influence the development of local projects and national networks in these young democracies.

Profound cultural differences derive from the years of state provision and state influence. This has generated a widespread over-reliance on professional services, an expectation of 'being told what to do', and a lack of belief in the concept of confidentiality. This can make callers reticent about a service based on volunteers and 'listening'. An additional problem is that in some countries suicide is illegal, so both counsellors and callers are deterred from discussing the subject.

> Because of the last 70 years of their history, during which period people had to do as they were told, it was sometimes difficult to get away from the idea of giving advice. *(Ken Blakeley, BI volunteer on a visit to CIS, Befriending World-wide, November 1992)*

The different cultural and legal norms may make it difficult to promote the BI approach, and the formation of a BI national association may be difficult since this could challenge the existing networks of providers that are using a different set of principles and practices.

> The centres are staffed by psychiatrists, psychologists and social workers. To British eyes, their location in the psychiatric department of large hospitals may be seen as a disadvantage ... but it may not appear so to the Hungarian caller who, we are told, believes that their crisis can only be resolved by a highly-trained specialist. *(BI report on a visit to Hungary, 1992)*

There are also a number of practical difficulties that may inhibit the establishment of BI-type services. In Eastern Europe there appear to be particular problems in finding adequate accommodation. Existing services often operate from one room, making confidentiality problematic. In some areas, physical isolation and an inadequate telephone system are key issues. The cost of living is also a barrier to a service based on volunteering. To survive, many people have several jobs, and it is impossible to operate a service without paying the 'befrienders'. Finally, visitors have noted the absence of training facilities – chalkboards, flip-charts, overhead projectors, video machines – that may be taken for granted by UK-based staff accustomed to UK training contexts.

The programme of visits and exchanges with Eastern Europe is continuing. For BI this is an essential part of achieving its mission, and a learning process that will help it develop in other parts of the world (such as China) where it currently has no presence. Of equal importance is the positive impact for the individuals involved: for both the UK volunteers and their European partners the process of exchange and joint working is challenging and rewarding.

The UK visitors to Eastern Europe have obviously been touched by the scale of need and the lack of resources, training and support. However, this offers a significant challenge to BI. The need for its experience and support appears to be obvious, but several of the basic principles and practices that are fundamental to its approach do not fit easily with the current organisational and cultural norms of its Eastern European partners.

> I feel that BI should continue helping organisations in the CIS whether or not they are BI centres. It has 40 years experience behind it and is the only organisation able to provide what is needed. *(Ken Blakeley, BI)*

3.2 Groundwork Foundation – co-operative action to solve environmental problems

With a research and development grant from the EC Environment Directorate-General (DGXI), and the support of BP and ARCO Chemical, the UK-based

Groundwork Foundation was able to undertake initial work in several European countries and run a conference in the period 1988–90. The project was called 'Groundwork for Common Action in Europe'.

The Foundation had several motives for promoting its approach in Europe. The first is a sort of missionary zeal: a belief that there is a role in other European countries for urban and urban-fringe environmental improvements, and a belief that the partnership approach would provide a good vehicle for local environmental projects. These beliefs arise in part from the enthusiasm and commitment to the Groundwork activities in the UK, in part from the interest shown by ARCO Chemical in establishing a project in Belgium, and in part from the interest shown in the approach by the European Commission. In practice, the development process tested the applicability of the UK approach in a range of European situations.

> It has been a widely held belief amongst the Groundwork staff involved in European work that there are tremendous gains from cross-fertilisation of experience between UK and mainland European practitioners. We have learned valuable lessons which have informed our UK activities.
> *(Walter Menzies, Groundwork Associates, Knutsford)*

A second motivation was to mirror the growth of a pan-Europe perspective within the private sector corporations that are major sponsors of the Foundation's UK work. This is perhaps linked to a third motivation which was to broaden the funding base for Groundwork activities – in part by gaining access to European Commission funding and in part by attracting additional corporate funding for their European work.

Underlying all of these motivations may be a subjective desire to embrace Europe – to see the Groundwork approach and activity in a European context rather than just an English context.

The development process consisted of seven feasibility studies – in Belgium, France, Ireland, Italy, Germany, the Netherlands and Portugal. Six of these were funded by EC DGXI and BP, and one by ARCO Chemical (Belgium). This work gradually built up the credibility of Groundwork within the European Commission by the delivery of the studies and a conference on time and within budget.

Four of the EC-funded study areas were suggested by the EC because of existing contacts. These were Lille (France), Essen (Germany), Terni (Italy), and Nijmegen (Netherlands). Two further sites were suggested on the basis of Groundwork's own contacts between Bristol and Oporto (Portugal) or convenience (Dublin). ARCO has a substantial plant in Evergem in Belgium where they wanted the study they funded to be undertaken.

> There is growing recognition that public sector agencies cannot deliver on everything and it was gratifying at Evergem how local entities

responded to the partnership concept. *(Clive Wright, ARCO Chemical)*

Although the selection of feasibility study locations was somewhat random, they nonetheless provided useful insights into two core questions:

- Are there environmental problems that would respond to the Groundwork approach, ie the creation of sustainable natural habitats?
- Does the partnership model – with local leadership and the involvement of government, business and the local community – offer a suitable way of tackling local environmental problems?

In June 1990, reports from the study areas were brought back to a conference at the European Commission in Brussels.

The research was undertaken by experienced staff from existing UK Groundwork Trusts and co-ordinated by a consultant to the Foundation. Although there was little co-ordination of research methods, a common approach emerged involving:

- desk research – gathering information about the locality and establishing contacts (with the help of the EC and the British Embassy);
- visiting the area and talking with initial contacts in the public and private sectors, and people already engaged with environmental issues.

Since the EC funding was in two phases it was possible to do second visits to three of the sites. Here the first visit helped to identify a 'local champion' (with detailed local knowledge and local credibility) and potential project activities. This knowledge enabled the second research visits to be more focused.

The 'unstructured' research process appears to have been appropriate since there was so little local information available from the start. It also suited the working method – identifying problems and then solutions – used by the Groundwork staff in their normal UK activities. Asking questions (rather then presenting solutions) also helped to build the credibility of Groundwork and the locally-based approach that they promote. The principal weakness of the development process was its under-funding. With a budget of just over £5,000 for each piece of local research it was impossible to spend enough time locally, or for the research teams to spend time together. This restricted the research work and constrained follow-up activities.

More care could have been taken over the selection of locations. However, the gathering of information upon which to make a more informed choice would have demanded substantial initial research. The EC-funded work was, in practice, a way of doing this research and identified a significant range of issues that should be taken into account in selecting any future sites for feasibility studies.

Although there was strong support for continued development from each location – since there were very significant problems to be tackled and an interest in the approach that was so successful in the UK – there has also been a recognition that there are significant barriers to developing a partnership approach and/or getting resources to work in several of the localities. Local projects are now under way in Lille (but without significant private sector involvement) and Evergem, and it is expected that a project will be established in Nijmegen.

Groundwork have drawn two general conclusions from their experience of developing into Europe:

- It is far easier to export objectives than methods of achieving them.
- It is very expensive and the process needs substantial resources.

However, the experience has also highlighted a number of factors that inhibited or enhanced the potential for replicating Groundwork projects in different locations. These factors are likely to be relevant to the transnational transfer of projects or approaches in any field.

The first factor is the priority given to 'the problem' locally. The Portuguese and German locations represented two extremes. In Oporto, basic environmental services – water supply, sanitation, waste disposal, and control of industrial pollution – were not yet in place, so little priority was likely to be given to the type of environmental improvements conventionally undertaken by Groundwork. In contrast, in Germany the awareness of environmental issues and the development of controls and regulations in this field left little scope for trail-blazing initiatives. So it is essential to ask if there is a demand for the service the project could supply, where demand is both a need and a willingness to allocate resources to satisfy it. If there is a demand, then it may be in one niche within the whole field of activity (for example, environmental improvements). The Trusts in the UK were developed to fill this particular niche, but in other countries the niche may well be different.

Where there is scope for Groundwork-type environmental work, it is important to find out who is expected to take responsibility for tackling these problems, what is their normal approach, and how open they are to new ideas. The studies were revealing:

- In Germany and Italy the expectation was that the State (centrally and/or locally) would play the major role, but in quite different ways: in Germany the State produced and policed environmental controls; in Italy there were few controls but the State was expected to lead any environmental action (and this tended to be high-profile buildings or public art).
- in Belgium and the Netherlands there appears to have been some acceptance that local firms (and they were typically multinational firms) should take a lead in 'cleaning up' the local environment – as an act of public responsibility and/or good public relations; in Germany, France and Italy this concept was not understood by local firms (although in

15

Germany, legislation placed the major responsibility for commissioning environmental work on firms).

- Only in Belgium, France and Ireland was there an expectation that community-based organisations had a role to play in the design and delivery of environmental projects.

These differences determined how much work was needed to get a local Groundwork-type project established: it is notable that the initial European projects are in Belgium, France (without a private sector involvement at present), and the Netherlands, and that development elsewhere is seen as much longer-term.

Local conventions or legislation about who should undertake the different roles in tackling environmental problems (for example, setting and monitoring standards, initiating works, carrying out works) will determine the flow of resources for the work. In Germany the prime responsibility for commissioning work lies with the 'creators' of the problem – typically private companies who contract specialist firms to carry out the work. If the state initiates work, then it expects to contract it to specialist private sector firms. In the Netherlands (as in Britain) the state commissions large-scale environmental works, but typically uses private contractors to carry this out.

The openness to change in the different countries reflected different legislative traditions. In Belgium, France, Ireland, Italy, and the Netherlands the legislation is permissive: the State can play a major role in environmental works and the methods it adopts are not set down. This allows people to be open to innovative approaches, although to achieve a change of tack may require agreement with several tiers of government and a lot of campaigning! In Germany the legislative tradition is far more directive: who must do what, in what way, is enshrined in legislation and is therefore more difficult to change. In Portugal, a young democracy, the legislative traditions are still developing and therefore the allocation of power between institutions is rather jealously guarded. Although there ought to be flexibility, there is instead a tendency to treat new approaches with suspicion.

Through the feasibility studies, Groundwork has been attempting to export both an objective (a natural and sustainable approach to urban environmental improvements) and a means of achieving it (the partnership approach). The feasibility work generated enthusiasm within the areas visited. This carried through into the 'feedback conference' at the European Commission where, despite the local problems revealed in the individual location reports, there was support for the development of a European Network of Groundwork-type projects. It is hoped that this will go beyond 'inspiration and information' by enabling local development. This suggests that 'European development' should start with pilot projects within each country which then lead to the creation of national networks and national development organisations. This is in contrast to a process based on the 'franchising' of a UK model.

The Groundwork concept has been tested in a variety of different circumstances and has been proved to be a robust idea that has something to offer in most cases. *(Patrick Leonard, Executive Director, Macclesfield & Vale Royal Groundwork Trust)*

3.3 Early conclusions

A lot of detailed research is needed to establish how copy-cat projects can be set up in another country. This is equally true for commercial organisations, although in that world there is more potential for buying-in packaged 'market information'. The Groundwork conclusion (following their feasibility studies) is similar to the approach taken by many multinational companies: if you want to expand into a 'market' that is subject to local legislation, expectations and traditions, then you need a local agent that is already well informed and well connected. In Lille this was the existing consortium of environmental groups; in Evergem, ARCO Chemical could play this role; while in Nijmegen it was provided by a local academic. Nevertheless, the existence of a 'local champion' is unlikely to be sufficient to carry a local project forward on its own.

In respect of the 'partnership approach' it is of particular importance whether the existing legislative framework provides for not-for-profit forms of organisation. Groundwork found that all of the feasibility study countries except Portugal had such frameworks, although in Italy, Germany and the Netherlands it was not used in ways that would easily facilitate a Groundwork-type partnership for environmental work.

The Groundwork experience has revealed:

- the need to have detailed knowledge of the receiving context and adjust both the objectives and the delivery mechanisms (including organisational design) accordingly;
- the importance of building on a local base of information and support;
- the high costs of undertaking local research and project development in another country.

3.4 Large companies and transnational giving

Further research sponsored by Corporate Community Investment in Europe on transnational giving by multinational companies has identified a role for major world companies in promoting the 'export' of projects they sponsor. ARCO, for example, has been an active partner in helping to develop

Groundwork projects, first in Belgium and then in France and the Netherlands, in regions close to company plants. IBM United Kingdom has developed a number of management training programmes for senior managers in the voluntary sector, originally using training methods developed for IBM staff and delivering the courses through their own trainers. This is now one of the projects that IBM has decided to develop world-wide, and an IBM operation in another country can apply to IBM United Kingdom for technical help in setting up a programme.

American Express had a travel and tourism project in the Bronx, New York, and discovered that it motivated non-achieving children, resulting in higher levels of school attendance and enrolment in further education. This scheme was then replicated in Britain, and subsequently Hungary and Russia. Most of the very large world companies have one, or even several, projects in their portfolio of community support, where they have taken a lead in their creation and of which they are particularly proud. The opportunity exists for the project organiser, in partnership with a counterpart in another country, and with the support of the company in both countries, to develop the project elsewhere, suitably adapted to meet local needs and conditions.

4 *Importing from Other European Countries*

The UK voluntary sector has no monopoly on good ideas, sound projects or far-sighted strategies. The successful transfer of the Foyer concept from France to Britain is described below. This is followed by a description of the activities of Age Concern Spain in Majorca, which is an 'import' because it has been set up at the behest of local residents, not deliberately 'exported' by Age Concern England.

4.1 The Foyer experience – replicating a French organisational concept in the UK

The Foyer concept has been developed in France since the 1950s, where there are currently 450 projects offering accommodation for 100,000 young people each year. They were originally conceived as a way of facilitating the free movement of young workers at a time when industry was expanding; more recently they have played an important part in combating young homelessness.

> A Foyer is an integrated approach to meeting the needs of young people during their transition from dependence to independence by linking affordable accommodation to training and employment. *(Foyer Federation Good Practice Handbook)*

In France the Foyers are linked through a strong network (Union de Foyers pour les Jeunes Travailleurs – UFJT) which started to campaign in the EC on the issues of youth homelessness. They researched and published a study of youth homelessness across Europe, and the contact made through this process led to the establishment of the European Organisation for the Integration and Accommodation of Youth (OEIL). The French network provides the co-ordination and secretariat functions for this European network. Shelter was the first UK member. There are member organisations from Denmark, Germany, Greece, Ireland, the Netherlands, Portugal and the UK.

The development of Foyers in Britain occurred through several initiatives:

- London and Quadrant and North British Housing Associations had contact with the French network and, in partnership with the YMCA (Young Men's Christian Association), approached the Housing Corporation with a proposal to establish seven Foyers (two of them new, five YMCA conversions) in Britain.
- Shelter and the Housing Corporation launched a competition (with a single prize of £1 million capital funding) for the best Foyer proposal. This stimulated 40 bids. Additional prominence was achieved by making the design of the Foyer the subject of an architectural competition: although this produced some problems for the winner (who had to finance a winning design!), it gave the Foyer concept a high media profile.

Many of the Foyer proposals submitted for the competition have since been initiated anyway, contributing to a current development programme that will result in 42 projects operating by the end of 1995.

The rapid implanting of the Foyer concept into Britain has been aided by the early establishment of the Foyer Federation for Youth, by Shelter and the private company Grand Metropolitan. This established a coalition of housing associations and economic development organisations (each bringing their own ideas and experience) and provided a base for staff secondments from government departments. The latter provided the essential links back to public policy. The Federation has helped promote the Foyer concept and has developed training and 'good practice' material. It is also a key member of the European network and the route for feeding ideas from a wider range of countries into Britain.

In many cases the Foyers in Britain are being established and managed by the YMCA, possibly using existing buildings that are upgraded in partnership with a housing association. There have been some significant gains from replicating the French concept into Britain:

- Foyers are perceived as innovative. This has resulted in an increase in the government funding available to tackle an acknowledged problem which was previously given a low priority in UK public policy.
- Establishing the links between accommodation, economic opportunity and personal independence is important: in Britain the links have been known, but too often the services have been delivered in separate ways.
- By giving equal weight to 'training and employment' and 'progression to independence' the Foyers will begin to challenge the operating culture that has emerged in some existing youth accommodation providers, a culture that is perhaps 'over-protective' and can institutionalise residents.

- The attention given to this multi-faceted approach, and the formation of a national information and co-ordinating body, has established links between numbers of projects that already existed, giving them all a higher profile, the prospect of additional funding, and opportunities for mutual learning and support.

Although the French concept has been 'imported', the organisational and funding arrangements for Foyers in Britain have been tailored to the local context. For example, in France the public sector has provided most of the capital funds and continues to provide a 20 per cent revenue subsidy to each project. In Britain the development programme is based on different assumptions:

- the capital funding is typically a mixture of public sector grants (Housing Corporation and local authority) and private sector lending;
- the training and employment activities usually rely on existing services and funding regimes, such as those offered by Training Enterprise Councils, Further and Higher Education Colleges and the Employment Services;
- both the public agencies and the private sector may support the initiatives via staff secondments.

There is also the possibility in the UK that a higher level of private sector involvement may give greater employment opportunities for the young people involved.

There are two dangers with this pattern of provision, which may have a long-term impact on the sustainability of the Foyers in Britain. First, the lack of public subsidy may result in rent levels that cannot be afforded by working young people. Using a mixture of public and private sector funding it is possible to establish a Foyer that is financially viable, provided that many young people are obtaining a student grant or housing benefit. Will these young people be able to afford to live in the Foyers when they obtain a job in a labour market that is generally suppressing wage levels?

> Over the last 30 years it has been the norm in the UK that if hostel residents do not want to work then they are not strongly encouraged to do so or given expert advice. To overcome these attitudes, the UK Foyers all incorporate job search provision . . . In France, because cultural and peer group pressures encourage young people to move into work and training, there is much less job search provision on site. *(Don Macdonald, Foyer Federation for Youth)*

Next, there is the danger that the Foyers, reliant as they are on resources from mainstream programmes that are based on pre-existing operational assumptions, will not succeed in establishing a distinct operating culture. The French model is not just a package of services, but the creation of a working method that requires the integration of professional cultures and skills – in housing management, counselling, training and job search. While the Foyers in Britain are utilising funding regimes that are not dedicated to their specific aims, then there must be a risk that the 'strings' attached to the funding will inhibit the development of an integrated operating culture, or indeed that the funding of the training and employment aspects of the project will be withdrawn when the focus shifts to the next 'innovative' idea!

4.2   Age Concern Spain (Baleares) – working with UK pensioners in Spain

Age Concern Spain (Baleares) is the local equivalent of Age Concern England for foreign residents who have retired to the Balearic Islands. Although it receives support from Age Concern England, like its UK counterparts it enjoys a substantial measure of autonomy. It incorporates OASIS (Overseas Association Social and Information Service), which began in 1988 in response to the problems of growing older abroad.

> We find people face all sorts of difficulties as they grow older. If a partner becomes very sick or dies, the one who remains often has no plans. For example, a widow loses her husband – who used to do all the driving – and she can't drive herself, and she can't speak the language. *(Judy Arnold-Boakes, President, Age Concern Spain)*

The services offered by Age Concern in the Balearics echo those available in many Age Concerns in the UK. However, they have been tailored to suit local needs:

- Lifeline, one of the organisation's core activities, is a network of contacts in government, medical and social services, and other areas of Spanish life; it seeks to assist those people facing more acute personal, health and financial problems.
- Tele-Alarm, working in conjunction with the Spanish Red Cross, provides a 24-hour, year-round telephone-based alarm system; the Red Cross control centre offers services ranging from instant emergency help through to meals-on-wheels or shopping for those who are temporarily too unwell to do it for themselves.
- CHAT is the Clinic and Hospital Action Team of visitors, all of whom are volunteers.
- The Information and Advice Service offers fact sheets and a telephone advice service.
- Training, which Age Concern conducts under a 'caring *for the carers*' banner, is for the volunteers who give advice or make visits.

Age Concern is thinking of running a mobile shop, complete with information service, in order to reach those people living in the more remote parts of the island.

The links with other voluntary organisations extend beyond the Spanish Red Cross to local branches of the Salvation Army, the Anglican Church, and so on. But, however necessary these personal social services, the organisation seeks to promote integration as the best way to improve the quality of life. They are now starting further initiatives to support this philosophy:

- Meeting points throughout the Islands, 'where people can "pop in" for a chat or a coffee', form part of the strategy for counteracting isolation and loneliness.
- Language teaching: on a reasonably light-hearted basis, a qualified teacher is about to start Spanish classes, at two levels (beginners and advanced).

The Age Concern publicity leaflet emphasises the European context throughout:

Age Concern Spain . . . is an international organisation, integrating foreign nationals into the Spanish way of life . . . with access to EC developments through Eurolink-Age. Eurolink-Age itself deals with all questions and problems of older people in the EC. It has valuable liaison with the Commissioners who are at the hub of affairs in Brussels. It is concerned with the experience and skills of older people which it feels could, and should, be put to good use.

One example of the impact of cultural differences is that many people from the UK find it hard to come to terms with the Spanish method of burial management: the dead are buried in a 'niche', somewhat akin to a filing cabinet drawer system, which is then cemented up, and may only be rentable for five years, after which the body and coffin are put into a common grave; the Spanish are also not accustomed to the family attending the grave at the burial. However, cremation is now available in Majorca.

Having sufficient money to live is a key issue. Many people retired to Spain some years ago, when the cost of living was much cheaper than in the UK. Now, if anything, it is higher in Spain than the UK. On top of that, people are living longer and low interest rates are affecting the income generated by investments.

The fluctuations in the value of the pound against the peseta a few years ago left some people very badly off. So much so, that we raised funds from UK benevolent funds and charities to help them. *(Judy Arnold-Boakes)*

For its income, the organisation relies on subscriptions from members, traditional fundraising activities, and runs a 'Friends of Age Concern' appeal.

5 *European Partnerships*

The third option for voluntary organisations wanting to become involved in European work is for mutual partnerships to be developed. This chapter's case study provides an insight into how these can grow to become a major part of an organisation's work, from quite modest and straightforward beginnings.

There are some imaginative and innovative partnerships being established. For many years there have been twinning arrangements between European towns and cities, often involving considerable voluntary sector input. But now there is also the United Towns Organisation (UTO, or Fédération Mondiale des Cités Unies et Villes Jumelées, based in France), consisting of local and regional authorities (towns, provinces and regions). It has 74 members, in Europe, French-speaking black Africa, Arab countries, Latin America and South-East Asia. UTO is developing technical agreements between towns, covering sanitation, transport and municipal management. It carries out audits and expert evaluations, and sets up projects with specific objectives, often in collaboration with the World Bank and the EC. It has also set up a United Towns Development Agency in the field of North–South co-operation.

5.1 East Anglian Co-operative Development Association – sectoral partners in Europe: fostering development

East Anglian Co-operative Development Association (EACDA) is a service co-operative concerned with the regional management of European Social Fund (ESF) programmes in the co-operative and community economic development sector. It also provides professional support services – joint training, marketing and promotional activities – to its members, mainly co-op development agencies based in Basildon, Luton, Cambridge, Colchester, Harlow and Norwich. It receives backing from county and district councils in the area.

Formed in 1987, EACDA quickly became involved in ESF transnational programmes, with its first ESF funding for training for long-term unemployed people accepted in 1988. The finance would not have been forthcoming unless the projects were transnational in scope: 'In order to get ESF funding, we had to find European partners' *(Rachel Sleet, Co-ordinator, EACDA)*.

EACDA and its members were not unwilling to get involved at European level. In fact, when Harlow CDA was established, the commitment to working at the European level was built in from the start. From 1990, it was no longer mandatory to have transnational partnerships for ESF funding for vocational training. However, the option of dropping European links was not taken up. 'We used the time allowed by this release of pressure', says Rachel Sleet, 'to establish more meaningful exchanges and potential partnerships with our European colleagues.'

Three EC initiatives – NOW, HORIZON and EUROFORM – provided EACDA and its members with an opportunity to take their ideas forward. Harlow CDA, through EUROFORM, was involved with a training initiative that looked at vocational training, training materials, training methodology and research, and the transfer of experience and good practice, with partners in Ireland, Italy and eastern Germany. Significantly, a good working relationship with two of the partners (in Ireland and Italy) had previously been established before the EUROFORM project came along, through the mechanism of study tours. EACDA now spends time deliberately fostering these 'prior relationships' between its members and colleagues in other European countries, so that they are ready to take advantage of EC initiatives as they come on stream.

Essex CDA, through the HORIZON programme, managed a large project, with backing from Essex Social Services Department, with a partner in Corsica (which has EC Objective 1 status). EACDA is convinced that local authority backing is essential for any project planning on spending money and resources on transnational activities. Rachel Sleet sees it as 'hard to convince funders that there are benefits to trainees, especially as the costs can be so high.' In the case of Essex, the senior officer responsible within Social Services was a member of the team who went out to Corsica to plan the project. This enabled the department to gain a close understanding of all that the project entailed and meant continued support from the local authority.

EACDA has encountered problems along the way, none of which are insurmountable. However, they stress that care needs to be taken with essentials:

- communication – not just language barriers, but the difficulties created by distance, different working hours, poor telephone or fax connections, public holidays;

- finding similar organisations – EACDA soon learnt that the co-operative and community economic development sector varies widely from one member state to another, and that it is not always easy to facilitate a useful exchange, because of differences in culture, size, funding, or even client groups;
- maintaining contact – continuity can be difficult, especially if your key individual contact within your partner organisation moves on, or even moves to another post within their set-up;
- funding preparatory work – a lot of time and energy has to be spent to develop worthwhile partnerships, and the amount of funding required for this initial contact is easily underestimated;
- project management – once the project is up and running, good management is necessary to make sure that declared objectives are met and accurate records are maintained.

Before embarking on a major programme, especially one which involves strict deadlines and targets, EACDA prefers to create a partnership through a pilot programme, an exchange of personnel, or simply a short study visit. Currently, through the EGLEI network (European Group for Local Employment Initiatives), EACDA members are sending three staff on week-long exchange visits to Italy, Greece and Spain. In due course, three people from organisations in other countries who are in the EGLEI network will be spending a week in East Anglia.

The benefits of the European experience to EACDA and its members are many and varied:

- widening the experience of trainees and trainers;
- staff and project development;
- innovative projects;
- exchange of useful information concerning working practices, marketing, targeting client groups, dealing with legislation; and, of course,
- new sources of funding.

Rachel Sleet hopes to 'see the benefits from the investment of resources in this work in terms of confidence, job prospects and future developments.'

Six years further on, European transnational projects and networks are a central part of the daily work-load at EACDA. The EUROFORM experience provided a solid foundation on which to build the European work of the association.

We find real flexibility in funding is at the European level; this is where projects are at their most innovative. *(Rachel Sleet)*

For some time, EACDA has 'avidly' collated information on Europe, keeping track of initiatives and developments for its members. Sources have included EUCLIDE, a weekly news sheet from Brussels that arrives via the Industrial Common Ownership Movement (ICOM) and the EGLEI network. Now, EACDA is about to launch a European information service that will be distributed more widely, to the local co-operative sector, economic and business development agencies, TECs and local authorities. It will also be accessing European databases through the recently established e-mail network, ARIES.

In 1991, EACDA published a booklet *'Linking Initiatives – How TECs and CDAs can co-operate'*, in conjunction with ICOM, the National Council for Voluntary Organisations (NCVO) and London Co-operative Training, which was distributed to every TEC in the country. It is used by CDAs to explain the extent and nature of their work, in terms of both enterprise development and training. Now, EACDA also provides an ESF consultancy and training service directed mainly at TECs and local authorities, who are looking at ways of maximising the money available for training. In this way, EACDA's European experience is being fed back directly into the local economy.

6 *Getting Going: Setting European Objectives*

6.1 An organisational strategy

To secure your European work, it is important that the commitment to it is independent of the individuals who have made the initial effort. There should be a written European strategy to which the whole organisation is committed. If you do not have one, there is a danger that the effort already invested will go to waste:

- the key staff members may move on to other tasks and priorities within the organisation, or
- they may leave the organisation, or
- there may be a lack of understanding of where European action fits into the work of the organisation as a whole; if it comes to be seen as a 'freaky, fringe activity' or as a 'gravy train for senior staff', internal criticism of the work can then put it at risk.

The whole organisation needs to start 'thinking European', in order to ensure that the European work is thoroughly rooted. The work should not be restricted to a few people or a specialist section, but knowledge and opportunities should be shared throughout the organisation, including:

- management committee members
- volunteers
- project users
- and staff at all levels

This will maximise the resources that you can bring to your European work and spread the benefits (direct and indirect) that evolve from it across a wider range of people.

The development of an organisational strategy will demand a rational examination of what you are trying to achieve and how you are proceeding. Early on, after you have gained some experience, it is appropriate that you stop and assess:

- how the European work contributes to the achievement of your organisation's goals;
- what you need to do to maximise the benefits to your organisation and the people associated with it;
- the organisational and staff development that needs to take place if you are going to achieve your strategic goals;
- potential sources of funding and other resources that can be pursued to help develop this work;
- a methodology for your work:
  - how to raise your profile in Europe
  - how to identify and work with partner organisations
  - how to establish 'branches' abroad
  - how to provide advice and support for European projects.

However, it seems likely that this strategy development is best done after some initial involvement in Europe, when you have some sense of what could be achieved and what the impact (both positive and negative) might be on your organisation.

> The main thing is to act. Do not waste time worrying over issues of co-ordination, or whether the thing in question has already been done. In the East European context, there is so much to be done, and so many others already acting, that to formulate grand and inclusive strategies will probably lead to frustration, dissipation of the interest and commitment of supporters and so no product. Obviously, you need to be aware and informed, but once the chance is there, act. (*James Jolly, The Prince of Wales Business Leaders Forum*)

6.2 Meeting local needs

A particular problem in Eastern Europe (and, no doubt, other locations) is the mismatch between the scale of local needs and what you feel you can provide. The scale of need in your particular field of activity may be so great that it can be intimidating: a feeling that is amplified by the range of needs in so many other related areas also.

In this situation, a pragmatic style of operation is necessary, and in any case fits in well with the development skills adopted by many UK voluntary sector organisations. It is worth being realistic:

- about what you can contribute and what local people can expect in the

short- and medium-term;
- about what you can ask your local partners to undertake.

It is critical to adopt a method of working that is appropriate for your situation. In all cases, it will move things forward considerably if you try to make sure that actions which have been agreed fit in with existing work-loads, ways of working and resource levels.

You should normally include an exit strategy unless you are establishing a branch that can continue indefinitely. The current 'conventional wisdom' is that UK projects working abroad should:

- be a catalyst for action rather than the actual delivery vehicle of the action;
- seek to develop a model that local people and local organisations can follow and develop.

The general aim is to enable local people to tackle local problems themselves. However, you need to be aware of the harsh economic and social climate in which local people may have to exist and the demands that this places on their time and resources. This mirrors the situation found in areas of high unemployment and deprivation in the UK. Here, it is often the people with a stable and relatively comfortable existence – because they are employed or retired – who get involved in community and voluntary activities. The unemployed and those dependent on meagre state benefits tend to be absorbed in the demanding process of 'getting by'.

European objectives: a checklist

Points to consider when drafting your organisation's European objectives:

Benefits to your organisation

- financial (eg another source of revenue or capital)
- learning from others' experience
- expansion or new area of operation
- co-operation and co-ordination on a broader front
- meeting your organisation's overall objectives
- satisfying the expectations of funders and supporters

Benefits to the people in your organisation

- staff development and training
- user involvement and participation
- management skills to be enhanced

Benefits to Europe

- financial (eg alleviate unemployment in poor region)
- learning from UK experience
- learning to live with each other
- learning about different cultures and languages

Risks being taken

- financial (eg cash flow overstretched)
- absorption of scarce resources that should be otherwise deployed
- failure of project
- placing too much strain on individuals and/or on the organisation.

7   *Getting Going: Establishing European Links*

7.1   Identification of existing contacts

You may already have the makings of a European project right under your nose. Many organisations start to work with European partners after making contact through existing staff, users and volunteers. An individual's enthusiasm is frequently the spur to making links, and personal contacts are probably the biggest single explanatory factor in the pattern of relationships between UK and European organisations.

One useful approach is to draw up a list of your in-house 'European resources':

- Who has knowledge of European languages?
- Who has travelled to which countries?
- Who knows about the different cultures and institutions within European countries?
- What contacts do people have in other countries?
- Who knows someone who can do translations?
- Who has photographs of similar projects in other countries?

Senior staff in community and voluntary organisations may, rather arrogantly, assume that it is amongst their ranks that this information will be held. This is not going to be the case: amongst the users or volunteers there will be people with close family links in another European country, and perhaps good knowledge of a European language. You may be surprised at quite how 'Europe-rich' your organisation and its local community is.

7.2   Established networks

Participation in UK-based national networks is, paradoxically, a good way to begin to grapple with the European dimension to your work. It is also a cost-effective and fast route into Europe for those organisations starting from scratch. It allows you to pick up the threads at your own pace, without having to travel abroad. Many UK national NGOs, such as Age Concern England, ICOM, local authority associations and NCVO, have well-established, direct links with similar bodies in other European countries and with European networks. In this way, contacts can be made relatively quickly and easily. For example, the Euro/International office of NCVO has a list of all the major UK voluntary organisations with specialist European officers.

If you have no contacts in Europe, then the first step could be to get involved in UK or European networks that cover your activities. The route into European networks is likely to be through a UK network or umbrella organisation. In many cases these are going to be task-specific or issue-based. Examples include the Pre-School Playgroup Association, Transport 2000, the Consumers' Association, Community Development Foundation and ICOM. Where the obvious networks do not exist, then it may be possible to find European contacts through national networking organisations like NCVO.

Other sources of information on contacts include:

- the excellent reference book, which lists dozens of European networks, *Networking in Europe: A Guide to European Voluntary Organisations* (by Brian Harvey, NCVO, 1992; new edition in preparation);
- European Information Centres (EICs), the official information providers of the European Commission and other European institutions, which are to be found in 222 major centres across Europe; they can be based in libraries, chambers of commerce and universities; your local library will be able to tell you where to find your nearest EIC;
- papers handed out at European conferences can be a good source of contacts, either by getting in touch with the event organisers (and asking them for names and fax numbers) or by going through the list of delegates;
- the EC official who has responsibility for your area of work and interest; find out if there is one and fax this person with your request ('I understand you are responsible for mutual and co-operative organisations: do you have a contact in a rural part of Portugal who is interested in building up credit unions for agricultural workers?'); explain who you are, why you need to know this information, and provide a reply fax number; as many EC *fonctionnaires* travel frequently, they may well be able to surprise you with how much they know; however, as they may also be on a visit to Greece or Denmark that day, please do not expect an instant response.

You can also talk with other projects doing similar work with which you are in contact. If they have a European link, then it may be possible for them to ask their contact for information on other similar European projects. Also, try local multi-sector networking bodies, such as your local CVS or Health for

33

All office.

Similarly, many local authorities now have full-time staff working on European matters. They tend to have modish job titles (such as, and this one is a genuine example, 'European Affairs – Human Resources'), but their location within the town hall structure gives the real clue as to their role. They are to be found in chief executive's or town clerk's departments, in the 'resource procurement directorate', or within the economic development department. Despite the intense pressure they face to wrestle money out of Europe for their borough, many of these local authority officers manage to sustain the altruistic or idealistic streak which lead them to seek the job in the first place.

Attending national conferences within your sector is another useful initial step, as a source of contacts and also as a learning experience in 'how to get the most out of conferences'.

7.3 Brokering services

An alternative method is to approach one of the brokering services that have been established to facilitate contacts between UK organisations and those in Europe, and between organisations throughout Europe:

- For Eastern Europe, Charity Know How (CKH) has established East–West Links and offers a contact point for UK organisations willing to provide support, and for Eastern European organisations seeking help. CKH is funded by the UK government to facilitate the development of the voluntary sector in the ex-communist Eastern European countries; CKH provides grant aid and advice, and arranges exchange visits, training programmes, conferences, workshops and seminars.
- The Euro-Citizen-Action-Service (ECAS) is a unique Brussels-based information and advocacy service which aims to strengthen the voice of voluntary sector associations within the European Union; it sees itself as the 'citizen's watchdog, aiming to create a better balance between public interest and corporate lobbying'; ECAS has developed an extensive database on European organisations, many of which are ECAS members; it also offers those organisations with slightly larger budgets a share in its Brussels infrastructure (office space and facilities, advice on EC contacts and lobbying, press conferences and so on).

An under-used route for making contacts is the town twinning arrangements which are operated through local authorities. Conventionally, these are concerned with social and cultural contacts, but they may be able to provide a point of contact within the local authority in their twin town(s), through which you can locate community and voluntary projects doing work similar to your own.

I first got involved by finding out, through the Tourist Information Office and the Mairie (Town Hall), the addresses of the five *écoles maternelles* in Coulommiers (our twin town in France) and then writing to the *directrices*. One responded and has remained a friend since. Through her introduction, I visited all the other *écoles maternelles* in the course of my exploration. *(Barbara Keeley, Leighton Buzzard)*

The concept of town twinning has been picked up by the Prince of Wales Business Leaders Forum as a mechanism for transferring know-how in economic development and employment creation from the UK to Eastern Europe. This economic twinning may be at town or county level.

8 *Getting Going: Information Exchange, Cultural Aspects*

8.1 The European political system

The post-1945 European structures and institutions are complex, and already laden with history. There are many publications and pamphlets available to introduce you to the new Europe, and this ground will not be covered again here. Suffice to say, in order to obtain funding, exert influence, or simply make the right connections, you need to identify the correct office desk and its occupant and to take time to build a relationship with the key officials, elected members of parliament, and their advisers.

Within the UK, you need to learn and use the appropriate (and, some would say, fashionable) jargon and terms, when you are pursuing grant aid and funding. The same applies in Europe, and as indicated elsewhere, these terms do not always translate well into English. There is a need to learn the full meaning of the new vocabulary as used at the European level. The golden rule is not to pretend you understand something when you have no idea what it means. Precisely because so much of what is going on in Europe is new and rapidly evolving, you will find most people with whom you are in contact are more than happy to explain a word or phrase. They are more tolerant and patient because they have been through the same learning process as you are embarking upon, possibly very recently. If in doubt, ask!

8.2 Getting a foot in the door

Another route into Europe is to obtain funding to undertake research or to promote research by running a seminar. The research might aim to examine the potential for establishing projects in other European countries similar to ones you already run in the UK, by identifying:

- the needs and gaps in provision
- the ways in which the service could best be delivered and funded
- existing service providers and potential partners

A seminar approach would rely more heavily on the exchange of information, with participants from each country describing their project and the context within which it operates. From this it may be possible to identify gaps in provision in one or another country and develop partnerships with local providers to develop suitable projects.

> In autumn 1989, in association with the Council of Europe and European Commission, we organised a major trans-European conference on community development out of which we developed the elements of a three-year strategy. The strategy essentially addresses the impact of the single market act and political and economic union on local communities in the UK and the need to promote citizen participation within this European Union through community development. *(Charlie McConnell, Community Development Foundation)*

This route often relies on European Commission funding, but obtaining this may require considerable work, including building a 'profile' both nationally and within the relevant directorates-general in Brussels. It can therefore require a significant investment of time and money (for example, for travel to Brussels). The demand for 'up-front' resourcing may mean that this route is confined to the larger and better-resourced community and voluntary organisations. However, it is still possible for smaller or local organisations to build a profile in Europe, usually by working closely with other projects, and with local authority support. Where campaigning, lobbying and representational work is involved, it is practical for small organisations to make an impact that belies the scale of their operation. Judicious use of electronic tools (fax, telephone and database) can be combined with careful targeting and good, clear copy to create a formidable presence.

8.3   Responding to requests

Any of the above approaches may stimulate a request for information or contact from an organisation in another European country. Initially, they may be interested in a group coming over to the UK to see how you deliver a particular service and to learn from your experience. This may develop into a more specific request that you provide training and expertise to the development of a project in Europe, or it could lead to European nationals spending a longer period in your organisation and then returning to establish a similar project within the cultural and institutional framework that they know well.

The gradual development of understanding and personal contacts between UK and European projects through training and exchanges provides an excellent base for subsequent closer working, for example, through the operation of 'parallel projects' funded by an EC programme.

8.4 Events: conferences, seminars, workshops

The content of a conference or other event may provide useful background information (such as changes to public sector funding criteria and regimes, changing legal contexts, different approaches to service delivery). But it is widely agreed that the informal contacts made at conferences are of more long-term use. So, participating in small group sessions, and being prepared to engage with a range of 'strangers' at meal times, coffee breaks and social gatherings, can be as productive as the formal proceedings.

At international events it is common to find many participants from other countries who are able to work in English. However, if you are attending a national event in another country, you will achieve much more from this if you can speak the local language. Many people attending these conferences – especially those from the host country – will not expect to work in English!

Lessons from European conference-going: a checklist

You ought to have a good reason for attending any conference, but especially so for European conferences (of which there are a growing number), where the costs and time of travel, but also language and cultural differences, make your attendance that much more difficult to justify.

Points to think about, before deciding to go:

1 Why is the conference being held? What are its aims? Are these relevant to you?
2 Why are you interested in going? What do you hope to get out of it? Can you set any clear objectives for your attendance? This might be to learn from others' experience, to share ideas on a common problem, or something more specific, such as to advance your chances of obtaining European funding, to obtain fresh material for a journal or publication, or to discuss setting up a joint project. Is there any preparatory work you might usefully do?
3 Are there people attending (including speakers) you might be interested in meeting?

4 Who else from the UK is going to be there? Are any of your 'rivals' or 'competitors' going? Do you need to be seen to be there? Do you need to be involved?

5 How much will it cost (including travel, hotels, and your time)? Are there special rates for voluntary organisations? Free places? Can you cut costs by finding somewhere to stay, rather than staying in the 3- or 4-star conference hotel? Have the event organisers arranged any rail or air travel discounts? Would it be better value, this time around, to buy the conference proceedings and stay at home (or attend the other European seminar with which this one clashes)?

6 Can you link it in with anything else? Are there other projects or organisations, perhaps doing similar things to your own, that you must visit? A double reason for going will make even more sense. Can you wear another hat? Is there another organisation that is unable to go, but would like to be present, and which will be delighted for you to take some literature over and find out specific points of information, make contacts and so on, on its behalf?

Points to ponder, when you are there:

1 Remember that not everyone speaks English! Do you have other languages? Will there be any translation services? If there are, will it be simultaneous, will it be for the whole event or just the plenary sessions, and will it include translation during any associated technical visits? Remember too that listening to translation through headphones for long periods of time can be quite tiring. And the translation is not always precisely what the speaker is saying!

2 Styles of conferences vary: not all are participative. The French seem to like long declamations by speakers without visual aids, broken up by long lunch breaks!

3 It is expensive for you to attend, so be certain it is worth while. Travelling abroad, especially if you are on your own, is tiring and demanding, if only because of the large amount of information that has to be rapidly assimilated; this means it is very tempting to slip unthinkingly into following the printed programme, without checking that it is meeting your goals. Yet you must be quite ruthless with how you spend your time. If you are there to meet people rather that to listen to presentations, then make sure that you do. If you have set yourself specific objectives, then make sure you make some progress towards them. If you find that you are not getting anything out of a particular session, and there is no prospect of you changing the situation, do not sit there feeling bored and alienated. Get out and visit a local project doing work that you are interested in; at the very least, go back to your room and freshen up, returning in time for the next informal point in the programme. If you intend taking photographs, do not skimp: you may only be there

once, so shoot two rolls instead of one, and think about whether you need the same shots on slides as well as colour prints.

4 It is very easy to stick with delegates from your own country; even easier to talk at length with close colleagues, if they happen to be there. However, meeting them in the UK would be much more sensible! If you meet someone from the UK who you do not know, be brief, get their card, and contact them when you get back home. Talk with the people you may never meet again.

5 If you are there, you may as well participate, so play an active role in discussions and panel question-and-answer sessions.

6 Bring along visiting (or 'business') cards. Pay some attention to the format of the cards: the address should have 'England', 'Scotland', 'UK' or whatever at the end; the telephone number should be in international format (+44 (0) 161 123 4000); and you must include a fax number (the key method of communication). Take plenty of information about your organisation and its work; it may be worth preparing a straightforward summary leaflet, say, a single side of A4, especially for the event; preferably with a version in the native language of the country which you are visiting.

7 You will receive lots of information about other people. Make a note of who they are, whether there is anything you have promised to send them when you get home, and what else needs following up in due course. Better still, make sure you do the follow-up. The best time to do it is the first day you are back in the office; otherwise it becomes a burden, as all the usual day-to-day cares begin to demand your attention.

Some of the worst conferences I have ever been to have been European conferences. Yet I have always found that there are useful contacts to be made, ideas to take back home, or even the beginnings of things that require joint work. *(Michael Norton, Directory of Social Change, 1994)*

If you are organising a conference and hoping to attract European projects then you need to take into account:

* the provision of instantaneous translation, either by professionals, or by 'pairings' (for example, a French speaker is paired with another participant who can translate from English to French);
* the need for plenty of time for social and informal contacts;
* the inclusion of a workshop session that focuses on 'next actions' which can be used to bond contacts between participants who have similar interests;
* the travel and accommodation requirements of the international delegates; careful choice of location (do not underestimate the draw of a 'tourist attraction'), good transport communications (including an airport), and several different grades of hotel, can all make the difference between someone deciding to attend or staying at home.

Organising a European conference: a checklist

Speakers

Write to potential speakers for the conference well in advance of the event. If you want to include information about their talk or their organisation and work in the conference pack, persuade them to give this to you about two months in advance of the event, so that the information can be typed up and, where necessary, translated.

Make sure that speakers understand and agree the basis of remuneration: their travel, accommodation, fee (if any), and whether they get to attend the whole of the event, should be discussed, agreed, and confirmed in writing. Horse-trading and payment in kind are a common feature of international conference organisation. In the right circumstances, you can still organise an international event even if you are on a low budget, provided contributors all pay their own costs!

Promotion and publicity

Decide whether to produce a single brochure inviting people to participate (and in one, two or several languages), or whether to produce separate brochures in different languages. One answer is to produce the leaflet in the main language(s) of the event, but include – in a suitably prominent place – a note, written in several languages, offering to provide a translation into these languages.

Reaching your target audience as accurately and cheaply as possible is the next challenge. Unless you have a sound international mailing list, it will be helpful to have energetic and committed partners in different countries to send out the publicity. Piggy-backing your leaflet with other organisations' mailings is worth considering, but bear in mind they will be more inclined to slip it in for free or at low cost if it does not weigh very much (less than 10 gms). Many European NGO networks have extensive databases: talk to them about what service they can offer you.

Simultaneous translation

If the conference is being conducted in several languages and you are providing simultaneous translation via interpreters, receivers and headphones, do a test run the day before to check all the equipment is in working order. A whole conference can flounder if the batteries on the translation receivers are flat!

Decide early on what languages will be used for the conference. There are many permutations, including:

- single language
- single language, with papers translated into other languages

- single language, with simultaneous translation for plenaries and other key parts of the event;
- full translation for everything.

Whatever you decide, make this plain on all the brochures and publicity: 'The conference languages are English and Spanish'.

If you are offering translation, English and French have tended to be the norm. However, this can upset people from other countries. The language of the host country is a must, especially as it will guarantee a better level of local participation.

Translation facilities are expensive. In workshops, costs can be kept down by having the interpreter whisper to those who need the translation or by having sequential translation (which can help instil some discipline in speakers, as it will encourage them to keep their contributions short and concise!). Either way, equipment will not be required.

Finance

Multilingual conferences are expensive to run. Participants will find it costly if they have to find a full-cost fee, as well as meet all the travel, accommodation and other expenses. You may wish to seek a grant or sponsorship for the event, to defray some of the costs or create a bursary fund to subsidise those participants whose organisations are badly funded (and who probably live in poorer countries, for example, in Eastern Europe).

Information packs for participants

Decide at an early stage in the planning of the event whether you want to produce one conference pack in one language, or in several languages; or varying packs in different languages.

Where the packs are in several languages, perhaps being put together with the assistance of partners in other countries, careful co-ordination will be necessary to make sure the same material is given out to everyone. It will be helpful to indicate whether or not you are going to publish conference proceedings afterwards.

Decide where it makes sense to have the conference packs printed. It is likely to be the country where the event is taking place. It might be advisable to arrive a week in advance to make sure the packs are going to be finished on time, as well as to co-ordinate any last-minute arrangements for the event.

Instructions on how to reach the venue

Participants should receive a map, with full public transport details, showing them how to get to the venue or registration point. Many travellers will find it useful to know in advance which kind of ticket to buy for the train, bus, coach or tube from the airport into town, and how much local currency they will need for this. Most large European towns and cities will have a tourist information centre, which can send you copies of an appropriate map, at low cost.

Hotel and flights

Offer one deal for flights and hotel accommodation to conference participants. You will be able to arrange the flights with a travel agency or airline, getting significant reductions for a large group travelling on the same flight; an accommodation deal should be practical with a hotel, or a college with vacant student rooms. Combined air and room packages from travel agents may be too expensive; it is definitely worth doing some initial research yourself. Different hotels, and flights leaving from different airports at different times, are a recipe for organisational nightmares.

If you give a participant's name to a travel agency or hotel, make sure it matches the name on his or her passport.

Participants may suddenly want to cancel their flight, or send a substitute: give them a clear deadline for making final changes to their flight arrangements and make it clear to them that after this time they must pay the total costs of the flight whether they attend or not. Agree the deadline with the travel agency or airline.

When organising a group flight, it is worth writing up a few instructions about how to reach the airport. It is especially helpful to mention from which terminal the flight departs.

8.5   The local context

While the local needs and problems may be similar to those experienced in the UK, differences in the legal, institutional and cultural assumptions in different areas of Europe may mean that you cannot 'export' your project to another part of Europe with any success. You can export goals, but be very cautious about exporting methods and organisational structures.

Experience would indicate that local implementation is best done by someone who understands the local context and has good contacts with key institutions at the local level. Where you are working with a local partner project, or providing training to local people, this may not be a problem since they will filter the information you provide and work out how to use it within the context that they know well. Where you are establishing a project in a European country, it may be more fruitful to recruit a local national and bring them to the UK to train them in 'your way', and then let them return to their own locality to set up the European project in a way that will achieve the objectives but fit with the local context.

8.6 The old colonial way

For many community and voluntary organisations in Britain that want to engage with Europe the objectives are mixed, but typically include a desire to learn from European experience, to access European funding, and to generate shared understanding between local peoples in Britain and Europe. However, other projects take a more crusading approach, believing that what they are doing in Britain can help resolve problems faced by local people in other European countries. There is a danger that this assumption might be seen by the intended beneficiaries as a form of neo-colonial oppression. Britain, like many other Western European countries, has some excellent experience of community and voluntary sector service delivery and campaigning organisations. It is right to offer to share this experience with local people in other countries, and perhaps especially in Eastern Europe where the community and voluntary sector is being rebuilt as the state sector is restructured, but this should be done with some humility. It is inappropriate to impose UK solutions on other people's problems.

8.7 Language

In Britain we have the advantage that English is a global language. You can get by in most areas of the world because somebody, somewhere, will speak English. Nevertheless, there are some fundamental issues around language that should be taken into account.

If you rely on local people's knowledge of English, you are effectively using language as a filter: you will effectively start to work with the better-educated, more cosmopolitan or more Anglophile of the local population. This may be a satisfactory starting-point so long as you are aware of the limitations which you have placed on your operation. A reliance on 'a universal language' is unlikely to be sufficient. If you honestly expect there to be a European element in your organisation's work-load, then UK-based staff need to learn to communicate in local languages.

Another barrier to good communication can be removed once you recognise that the meanings attached to English words are culturally determined. So even where you are working in English there can be very significant problems in comprehension. You may use the same words, but people from different cultures may attach different meanings to them.

As a more extreme version of this, there may be no local concept that could be attached to the language that you use – whether this is English or a local European language. We experience this, to some extent, in England when we try to understand terms that have been imported from Europe, such as 'the social economy', 'subsidiarity', 'exclusion' and so on. Here we can translate the word into English but, for many people, the English version has no obvious meaning. This is a problem being encountered in Eastern Europe where the historic domination of state provision means that many people do not have a concept of 'the community and voluntary sector' – or indeed, 'private enterprise'.

So the issues around language go much deeper than the relatively simple matter of finding an English-speaker when in Europe, or developing speakers of the local language in Britain. To some extent, these problems can be overcome by using a translator when abroad, but take care not to accept everything at face value:

- If you are totally reliant upon translators you are essentially giving them a high degree of power: they can change what you have said, filter what people say back to you, and control the person-to-person relationships that you are seeking to establish.
- If they do not have specialist knowledge of your activity and the UK context, they may have a weak grasp of the concepts that you are trying to convey; wherever possible, you should use a translator who knows your area of activity well and has spent a considerable period of time in the UK.
- If your European partners do not do things your way, then key concepts may not yet exist, making some words or phrases difficult – if not impossible – to translate; for example, in the field of corporate community involvement, the terms 'community investment programme', 'staff secondment', 'business leadership' or 'payroll giving' may be wholly unknown to a translator. Aid the translator by providing an accurate briefing beforehand, and – if there are a lot of technical words or phrases – supply a printed glossary of terms. If you have the resources and want to build up a good relationship with your translators, you can start by paying them an additional amount to prepare the glossary, for their own use, as well as yours.

On one occasion, in Eastern Europe, the translator who was being paid to help a UK group develop a local project was also accepting bribes from local providers of accommodation, food, and transport!

There are several mechanisms for translation:

- simultaneous translation, where the participants listen through headphones to a translation delivered as the speech is being given;
- in more intimate situations, a translator sitting behind you or a small group may whisper the translation into your ear as the presentation is being made;
- consecutive translation, where the speaker pauses frequently so that the last few sentences can be translated; this allows those with some grasp of the language to obtain a feel of what the speaker is saying, without missing any key points;
- translation of conference papers, so they can be read in advance, or whilst a speech is being made.

It is most worth while making an effort to participate in another European language. However small or token this may be, so long as it is done sincerely the gesture will be appreciated. The British have a reputation of only being able to understand English. When US President John F. Kennedy declared 'Ich bin ein Berliner!' during his visit to Berlin at the height of the Cold War in 1963, he correctly assumed this would make an enormous impression.

Whilst it may be true that more people at an event will speak reasonable English than any other language, people for whom English is not their mother tongue will respond warmly to your trying to use their language. In the longrun, if you are serious about working in Europe, you may wish to acquire another language. This may also be relevant when you are recruiting staff who will be engaged with European activities.

> I was invited to speak at a conference in Paris on promoting business involvement in social and community affairs. I prepared my talk in English, and asked a colleague at work to translate it into French. I then adapted the translation into my own French, which I delivered and circulated as a conference paper. My French, once semi-fluent, is now quite rusty. But the preparation for this talk helped me to recover my ear for the language, and I was able to participate in the discussion that followed. My efforts were much appreciated, and my stock went up with some of the seasoned European conference-goers present who had only heard me speak in English up until then. *(Michael Norton, Directory of Social Change)*

8.8 Training programmes

Language and cultural differences mean that you cannot easily transpose a training programme from one culture and language to another. So beware of simple assumptions here. A person translating material or delivering training needs a good technical grasp of the subject area in both English and the foreign language involved. Someone for whom the language you are translating into is their mother tongue will be preferred. There are also problems that arise from the incompatibility of qualifications in different countries, and potentially, difficulties that arise through very prescriptive regulations within the receiving country. Sources of advice on these matters include the National Council for Vocational Qualifications, the British Council, and a UK embassy of the country or countries in question.

8.9   Racism, sexism, discrimination

Both racism and sexism may be more overt in continental Europe than people from the UK voluntary sector are accustomed to. Disabled people may find there is even less acknowledgement of their existence than in the UK. When visiting or operating abroad it may become clear that there is little knowledge or understanding of equal opportunities policies and practices. UK projects, and in particular their non-white and ethnic minority participants, will need to be aware that the way people in other European countries deal with (or perhaps fail to deal with) these issues may be different. A strategy should be devised for dealing with this, if and when it happens.

8.10 Local cultures

One of the surprising features of working in Europe is the contrasting cultural assumptions in play. In turn, this leads to differences in the ways things are conventionally done. This can be stimulating and refreshing, but it can also be frustrating and can lead to misunderstandings that can threaten your European initiative. These cultural norms and expectations are rarely stated by the European project, and the starting-point for too many UK participants is that the British way is 'normal' and perhaps even best! Be prepared for differences in local assumptions in the following areas:

- *The role of the state* – Who is responsible for providing (and paying for) individual and societal needs? In the UK, which is out of step with many of its EU partners, the frontiers of state provision have been rolling back for nearly a generation. In mainland Europe there has been a general assumption that the state should and will generally provide for those in need. However, there are no hard and fast rules, because what is a public sector service in the UK may be provided by the individual, the church, the private sector, or through self-help groups in other countries, and vice versa. Before you know exactly who does what, be careful not to leap to conclusions.
- *Organisation* – How do you go about organising an activity? In some countries this is highly formalised – with decisions requiring endless meetings and everything carefully recorded – while in other countries it is extremely informal and relaxed.
- *Etiquette at meetings* – The formalities of running a meeting, conventions about room layout and time, and very different expectations about time-keeping, voting procedures and supporting paperwork.
- *Delegation and decision-making* – There are different expectations about 'delegated responsibility'; in some countries this is taken as a freedom to get on with the job in whatever way seems best, while in other countries it

is expected that there will be a higher degree of reporting back and joint decision making.

* *The work ethic* – The relative importance given to work, vis-à-vis non-work activities, such as eating, 'time out' and religious observance.

I was organising a workshop on the training needs of voluntary organisations at an ECAS conference in Montpellier, France. Discussion was lively and we continued beyond the scheduled break for lunch. I proposed that we limit the lunch break to ninety minutes rather than the allotted two hours. A French delegation rose as one person to say that this simply was not possible, and in the end we compromised by knocking quarter of an hour off. We then dispersed to local restaurants. By the time we had been fed and watered, we returned to the conference room two and a quarter hours later! *(Michael Norton, Directory of Social Change)*

While it is inappropriate to go into Europe with a set of stereotypical characteristics for each nationality – a stereotype which may be inappropriate for the people you are working with – it is important to recognise that differences exist and that they are not 'wrong'. It may be useful to discuss some of these differences and agree a pattern of working. Above all, when working in different cultural contexts, a flexible and open-minded approach is vital.

British organisations expect steering groups to send out details of what they are going to be discussing and canvass opinion, then circulate minutes to allow people to see what has gone on. Unfortunately, though the Germans may take the same view, other countries do not. For British organisations, the result for those not actually involved in the steering group can be a feeling of being ignored, patronised and unfairly ill-informed. But if they complain nobody can understand what they are going on about. *(Neil Hall, Urban Regeneration Consultancy)*

8.11 Travel in Europe

It has been emphasised earlier that European work should be spread throughout your organisation and include project users, committee members and volunteers, not just the senior staff. Exchange visits provide a useful format for the latter to become involved, but there are a number of common problems to watch for. The following points should be noted:

* Non-EC nationals may need to obtain visas to enter other European countries; within a local community it is not always clear who are UK nationals and who, although domiciled in the UK, are nationals of another

country, so it is worth finding this out in advance.

- Non-EC nationals should also carry copies of letters and other documentation from their UK organisation explaining the purpose of their visit.
- It is unfortunately true that black members of your group may get delayed when seeking to enter European countries or re-enter the UK; their documentation must be very clear and certain.
- Group members should carry their passports and other identification with them at all times; it is not unusual for people to be asked for identification (at borders, by public officials, bank clerks, the police), and a passport is a quick and easy means of satisfying this request. There is a convention at many of the larger multilingual conferences whereby you have to swap your passport or ID card for the simultaneous translation headphone sets.
- The security situation in Ireland can result in requests for identification, and passports should therefore be carried even though this is a 'common travel area' with the UK.
- It is useful to do some induction training on what people can expect from their hotel, covering, in particular, the local conventions in what are charged as extras, such as the bar in the room(!), the pay-for films on the TV and the extraordinarily high charges for telephone calls made from your room through the hotel switchboard.

Regarding the need to telephone home, by far the cheapest method for doing this is to use one of the proprietary telephone card systems (both British Telecom and Mercury offer an efficient service).

My favourite story is of a well-travelled colleague of mine who spent a week in Italy and on his return presented me with a laundry bill of £60. Each day the hotel had offered to clean his clothes: he thought his was tremendously kind of them – until he got the bill! *(Neil Hall, Urban Regeneration Consultancy)*

9 *Getting Going: Organisational Requirements*

9.1 Different legal frameworks

It is perhaps obvious that laws in different countries vary, although there is a steady move towards a common set of provisions within the EC countries, known in the jargon as an example of 'convergence'. What is less clearly recognised is that the legal traditions vary between countries. In Britain we have a relatively permissive legal system. Most 'legal persons' (including individuals and companies) can do anything which is not specifically excluded by law. Public bodies can only do what they are specifically empowered to do by law, but are often given considerable discretion about what they actually do and how they do it. In other countries the norm may be for very prescriptive laws, such as in France where the tendency is to codify the 'who' and 'how' elements of the function that is being given a legal framework.

There are two main definitions of 'non-profit-making organisations' which stem from two very different historical traditions:

1 The (Protestant) Anglo-Saxon tradition. Within this tradition organisations have very little defining structure; they have the legal capacity to carry out an economic activity; and they are able to distribute their assets. This is the case in Denmark, Alsace-Moselle, the United Kingdom, Ireland and to some extent Portugal.

2 The (Catholic) Latin tradition. Within this tradition organisations have a constitutional and legal structure defined by law or code: they do not have the legal capacity to carry out economic activity (and if they do, only after a long period of time); and they must be non-profit-making. This is the case in France, Belgium, Spain, Greece, Italy, Luxembourg and The Netherlands. In all these countries the

Napoleonic Code limits and rules the freedom of associations. *(Xavier del Sol,* Associations and Foundations in the European Community, *Directory of Social Change)*

In many ex-communist countries there is no well-developed legal framework (or even a language) for voluntary and charitable activity. This may mean:

- that it is difficult for people to conceive of what a community organisation, charity or not-for-profit organisation is;
- that it is difficult in practice to establish an organisation since there is no legal framework within which it can operate;
- that because there is a poor definition and few controls, the term community and voluntary organisation may be used inappropriately and may be brought into disrepute by bad practice.

Particular care needs to be taken in respect of money. Local conventions and legal requirements on accounting for money vary considerably. It is likely that you will have to account for money within the norms of the donor country, and this may mean setting up accounting requirements that are beyond normal practice in another country. Some UK projects have found it necessary to take full responsibility for accounting to ensure that this is done to the satisfaction of their financial backers.

The level of information on legal frameworks in the country in which you are intending to operate will be determined by the nature and scale of the intended activity. Where you are working with a local partner, you need to be aware of the legal context in which they are operating. If the intention is to establish a locally based project or a 'branch activity', then more detailed research will be necessary. This must cover both the legal requirements for establishing and managing an organisation, and the legal framework within which the particular service will be governed (for example, planning laws, minimum standards for buildings, equipment, staff, and so on). It is likely that you will need access to the knowledge and contacts of local people with experience in your particular field if you are going to obtain sufficient in-depth understanding of the legal context in which you are intending to operate.

The proposed European Association would help clarify the legal position of European-wide organisations. If agreed, it will provide a legal format to constitute organisations which operate within the EU and across member states' boundaries. Whilst this structure will be recognised in all member states, it will require incorporation in one particular country. There the organisation will be subject to the prevailing regulations and benefit from the available tax reliefs that apply only in that state. The European Association has been on the drawing board for some years now, making its way through the European legislative machinery at a snail's pace. Until it has been enacted, organisations wishing to operate in Europe will have to select one member state and register their organisation there.

9.2 Developing relationships

In practice, your work in Europe will be more successful if you find an organisation within your operating sector which:

- is working in a similar context;
- shares your goals and priorities;
- shares your belief in how problems should be tackled.

You should therefore consider your early partnership arrangements as a 'courtship' and avoid getting too deeply involved, too early. You need to be sure that you have a compatible partner.

In line with this, it is probably wise to start small and build up when you know more about the local context. It may help if you network with other UK organisations who are involved in Europe, sharing knowledge and experiences and thereby doing some 'mutual learning'.

In order to cope with your European work, you will need to build up your organisation's UK systems and personnel. If this is not done, then additional stress will be placed on hard-pressed staff and routines that were designed when there was only a UK project to manage, thus risking causing resentment within the organisation and criticism from key funders and supporters.

Try to ensure that there are opportunities for involvement (in the European aspects) for people at all levels within your organisation. This will maximise your access to people with relevant skills and knowledge, minimise resentment within the organisation, and provide the widest possible range of opportunities for people to experience 'being a citizen of Europe'.

9.3 Communications

References to the many obstacles to smooth communication are to be found throughout this book. There are ways of mitigating these problems.

The fax machine is not a luxury item for an organisation, or even an individual, working in Europe. Today, the fax is as essential to effective communication between two countries as the telephone on which it relies. Precisely because of different working hours, time zones, different public holidays and so on, it is now an accepted standard technique to preface your telephone call with a fax:

- State your business, including a brief summary of your organisation, your own position in it, and the questions, ideas or situation which you want to discuss.

- If you have not been in contact with the organisation before, ask for the name of the person dealing with this matter.
- State, using the international dial code (+44 for dialling from abroad to the UK), your own telephone and fax numbers, and when you will be at your telephone to receive calls.
- If there is a deadline, state why and explain the specific time or date by which a reply would be useful.
- If you are unsure about the contact, ask for a brief fax acknowledging receipt, and stating when would be a good time to ring to speak with the person directly.

The fax can beat a letter going by post by as much as a week. It is also ideal for reaching an officer of the EC, who may well spend significant amounts of time away from their Brussels office visiting other member states: when they return, the fax is there waiting for their attention. Finally, it is a (relatively) cheap way to make contact.

You need to pay attention to your telephone technique, if you are to avoid a large bill and frustrating or even embarrassing calls. It may be obvious that, before making a call, you should jot down the points you want to discuss; this saves time and money even when making local calls within the UK. But it becomes more important when making international calls. With language difficulties already in the way, it is critical that you are able to be concise about the matter in hand, and writing it down often helps to cut out any vagueness.

Information technology is rapidly enlarging the options for fast electronic communication between organisations in different countries. The cost of using these systems is now coming within reach of even the small, poorly-funded voluntary organisation. In particular, it is relatively simple to send a fax from a personal computer, using a fax-card inserted in your machine, or to use a modem to enable your computer to send and receive letters, reports and data down the telephone line to another computer. After a few false dawns and some years of development, electronic mail (or e-mail) systems are no longer the province of computer buffs and are emerging into the mainstream.

For example, ECAS and other European NGO networks obtained EIC status and finance in 1992 from the EC for ARIES, an on-line communication network for the social economy sector (or third sector). It is part of a vast electronic data transmission network called GeoNet. ARIES can provide access to a number of databases and information bulletins, especially those of the EC itself. This information can then be retrieved onto your own computer, after which you can go off-line again and read it, word process it, and otherwise manipulate it electronically, at your own pace. European NGO networks are planning to use ARIES for bulletin boards for their members, for finding project partners, and for information exchange and dissemination.

At the wilder shores of techno-babble, there is video conferencing, which – despite media hype – is still in its infancy. So far, it tends to be far too expensive for ordinary mortals (£750 per hour, plus the hire of rooms, equipment and the cost of the telephone links themselves). However, many large multinational companies have begun to cut into their international travel budgets by installing their own in-house video conferencing suites: perhaps you can persuade one to support your project, by allowing you an hour on their system to discuss matters with your colleagues sitting in similar suites in other European cities.

10 *Getting Going: Finance and Management*

10.1 Finance and resources

Developing a European side to your work will make substantial demands on both staff time and the revenue budget. You may find it wise to warn the accounts department in advance about some of the additional costs associated with activity at the European level:

- Travel budgets are – often literally – on a different plane, especially if you have no alternative but to book a peak-time 'business' flight; the cheaper methods of travel typically take longer and are at less convenient travel times.
- Because of the travel required, working in Europe can consume large amounts of labour time for a relatively modest time spent 'on site'.
- Exchange rate fluctuations can be problematic, and moving money internationally can take time and be expensive; paying by credit card is a good way to avoid changing large amounts of cash into other currencies, and it also helps the cash flow.

It is often difficult to raise money for working in Europe from within the UK. Both private sector and charitable funders are primarily concerned with the delivery of services in Britain and will need to be convinced that there is some domestic benefit to be derived from examining European experience. They are not usually keen to pay for visits to the UK by people from elsewhere in Europe and may be reluctant to cover the UK administration costs associated with European work.

The EC has probably been the largest source of funding for European work. However, this can cause massive cash flow problems, due to the way that grants are administered and paid. For the Structural Funds and certain other grant aid programmes, which are major sources of funding, usually over half of the costs have to be met from other public sources.

Moneys are paid in three stages: the First Advance is for 50% of the ESF (European Social Fund) allocation; the Second Advance for 30% (this can be claimed once the applicant has spent 50% of the First Advance); and the Final Claim pays any balance due following the submission of a Final Claim form. Although the best payment cycle would be January/ February (First Advance); May (Second Advance) and October of the following year (Final Claim), applicants should be aware that there have been severe delays in the past. *(from* European Social Fund – A Guide to Applying through the NCVO Programme, *NCVO, 1994)*

ECAS published a good guide to the main sources of EC funding (known as 'budget lines') in October 1993, called *A Guide to EC Funding for NGOs, the EC's Most Colourful Flowers.*

In most ex-communist countries there is almost no money available within the country for outside groups, and little money to pay the travel costs of people visiting West European projects. However, the British government's Foreign and Commonwealth Office has funded Charity Know How to provide funding for visits in either direction. According to CKH's *Notes of Guidance for Applicants*, grants can be made available for:

- advice on the legal, financial and regulatory framework necessary for voluntary organisations to operate effectively;
- advice and support for co-ordinating bodies seeking to promote and represent the voluntary sector;
- exchange visits between voluntary organisations in the UK and their counterparts in Central and Eastern Europe, the Baltic states and republics of the former Soviet Union;
- training programmes for voluntary sector personnel;
- conferences, workshops and seminars.

Funding is available for travel and subsistence and for the administration of programmes in the UK, but it is not available for teaching English as a foreign language, the administration of schemes for UK volunteers, core funding of projects in the region or in the UK, or the provision of offices or equipment.

The Foreign Office also has its own Know How Fund, for the transfer of expertise on economic development to Eastern Europe. Voluntary organisations may find that they qualify. For example, the Charities Advisory Trust has recently run a European symposium on museum shops. A European source of funding for the same purposes is the PHARE programme.

It may be possible to obtain financial support from companies, especially those that are active – or hoping to set up – within the area where you are intending to work. However, you need to be aware that they are looking for a positive impact for themselves (good public relations) and will not support politically sensitive work.

In most cases it will be appropriate that you adopt a modest lifestyle when abroad, especially when in areas such as Eastern Europe where there are high levels of poverty and deprivation. This can help to reduce costs. There are also benefits to be obtained from staying in people's homes when abroad. Apart from reducing costs, it helps to increase your understanding of the local situation and the context in which your project is operating. Exchange visits between groups of users and volunteers can be usefully arranged in this way.

When working in Eastern Europe and other areas in economic crisis, it is necessary to appreciate that local people simply do not have any money. The volunteers who you work with in the locality may find the postage and telephone costs of communication with you a very significant burden, and when people visit the UK they may have almost no cash. Particular care needs to be taken in these circumstances.

There is very little non-governmental funding available from overseas sources. Most grant-making trusts are limited by their constitution to making grants in their home country, and even where they are not, their particular interests and knowledge may effectively limit them to doing this.

The European Foundation Centre acts as a focus for foundations in Europe to meet together and share matters of common interest. Few of the foundations in membership from other countries will be making grants to bodies in the UK. The Centre has published two directories: profiles of the foundations that are members of the Centre, and a directory of foundation giving in Central and Eastern Europe.

Companies operating internationally may well have grants programmes in the main countries where they operate. They will be particularly interested in making grants for projects in those areas where they have a commercial presence – the nearer the project is to their factory or office, the better – or in those countries where they are hoping to develop their business. Usually, a local manager will have the responsibility for deciding or advising on grants. When considering grants, many companies may be looking for one of two things – good local publicity for the company or its projects, or to lend support to projects which somehow involve their employees (as beneficiaries in some way, as donors, or as volunteers).

In 1991, the Directory of Social Change (DSC) was asked to undertake some research into the practices of companies in Europe with respect to corporate giving and sponsorship. This covered overviews of all member states and 20 company case studies. To coincide with the publication, DSC organised a conference in Brussels to encourage companies to learn from the practice in other countries. Further information gathering and exchanges followed, leading to the appointment of a full-time co-ordinator – paid for from grants received for the project. This was then developed as a European initiative, based in mainland Europe. Through the support of the European Foundation Centre, the activity was transferred to Brussels to be run by them, and a business committee operating within the EFC has been established (called Corporate Community Involvement in Europe).

10.2 Time and timetables

It takes a long time to become aware of, and adjust to, the different cultural, legal and organisational frameworks within which you are seeking to work. So projects need to be set in a long time-frame. Funding arrangements rarely take account of this need for time for 'cultural adjustment'. Sometimes, the European work is seen as 'going out to provide expertise', without any appreciation of the reality that this expertise needs to be tuned to the local context if it is going to be of significant benefit.

Experience suggests that it takes much longer to establish an overseas operation than might be expected. A period of six to nine months, and quite possibly much longer, must be set aside. If you are setting up a base in Europe, and especially in Eastern Europe, then the initial six months or more may be absorbed in finding and equipping accommodation, making contacts, and beginning to understand the legal and cultural context. Take the long view, if you want the project to deliver real value. Do not underestimate the amount of time you need to allow for travel and make sure this is costed into the programme at the outset.

The length of the commitment and the time needed to get established may be seen as a barrier to involvement in Europe. However, those who feel it is essential to be working at a European level see this as an argument for getting started: accept that you are going to develop by a process of 'muddling through' rather than a carefully structured and pre-determined strategy.

10.3 Staff training and support

The seminars that preceded this book gave an indication that few organisations have given sufficient time and consideration to the training and support needs of the staff they are sending into Europe. This can be particularly unfortunate where people are going to potentially high-stress areas (for example, in Eastern Europe). Some voluntary sector workers who have spent long periods developing projects in Eastern Europe have talked of the traumatising effect of the experience, which can even lead to family break-up and personal crisis.

There appears to be little existing experience of a structured approach to staff training and management for people going to Eastern Europe. But thought needs to be given to induction training (including language classes), on-site support and management, and de-briefing and re-orientation when returning to the UK.

10.4 Personal development

When evaluating the benefits of European action, it is frequently reported that involvement in Europe is an enriching and stimulating experience for the people involved. Where client groups can meet and exchange experiences there is a breaking down of the sense of isolation, and an understanding that their problems are not unique.

Developing a European connection provides plenty of openings for staff development. The need to cover brand new functions – both abroad and in the UK – 'loosens up' the organisational structure, allowing some staff to move into fresh activities and others to fill the posts vacated. For people who have been 'stuck' in the organisation, possibly because of the lack of expansion within the UK, the chance to explore these opportunities remotivates them and brings forth energy and enthusiasm for their work both in Europe and the UK.

European work can also stimulate people throughout the organisation to learn (or re-learn) a foreign language, and it will give increased respect (and opportunities) to employees at all levels who have a foreign language skill.

Working in unfamiliar contexts means that you have to abandon some of your routine certainties and listen to others to find the appropriate way of working. Once again, this is a skill that can be usefully applied in the UK, especially in a period of very significant change. By listening, and understanding why people do things in a different way, it will help you recognise that you can be different, but equal.

Finally, senior managers report that the need to describe the work of the organisation, its rationale and context to new funding providers and to a non-English speaking audience has led them to re-examine the work of the organisation and improve their presentational skills. This is of benefit to both the organisation and the individual, in Europe and in the UK.

The experience of working on the 'Groundwork for Common Action in Europe' development programme has had a considerable training benefit for the Groundwork staff that have been involved. Speaking personally, leading a workshop on developing project programmes, conducted with French, Dutch and Belgian colleagues, was one of the more demanding experiences of my working life! I found that it forced me to think hard about my own work and to find particularly clear ways of describing it. It has also provided insights that have, I believe, helped me to do my job better. *(Patrick Leonard, Macclesfield & Vale Royal Groundwork Trust)*

10.5 Organisational development

Encountering the way other countries deal with problems similar to those you are tackling can lead to a re-evaluation of your own activity, specifically:

- what you do and why;
- what you say about what you do and why;
- your success and how it is measured;
- how worth while your current activity is.

This process can lead to fresh strategies within the organisation, and perhaps a renewed commitment to its ideals and to achieving them.

The exchange of information and ideas can lead to the introduction of different approaches to your work in the UK, using new technologies, techniques and practices. It may also lead to joint action on lobbying and campaigning at a European level, which could bring more resources and an improved context for work within the UK.

The introduction of new funding sources to work in Europe, or through a partnership with a European project, may allow you to extend your services in the UK at a time when funding opportunities for growth are very difficult.

Seeking and obtaining funding for your European work also has some indirect benefits:

- It will increase the fundraising experience and capacity of the organisation.
- It raises the profile and credibility of your organisation, which will help maintain and extend your resource procurement for your UK activities.

10.6 Measuring the benefits

It will be clear from the above that many of the benefits of involvement in Europe to the domestic organisation and the services that it provides will not be immediately measurable. There will, it is hoped, be some short-term gains:

- new funding obtained;
- information about new ways of working;
- staff and users excited and remotivated, generating commitment to the organisation and its work;
- a sense that the goals of the organisation, where these include or demand a European connection, are being achieved.

However, experience suggests that many UK organisations embark on their European experience with only a dim sense of the long-term benefits this would bring to the organisation.

Getting going in Europe is clearly hard work and requires determination and a will to let experience and involvement grow over a period of time.

There is an immense wealth of experience held in organisations all over Europe which can be of use to us in the UK and in turn we may have a lot to pass on to our European colleagues which we may be unaware of until we develop these partnerships. There is a willingness to make this type of partnership work which makes the problems surmountable. *(Rachel Sleet, East Anglian CDA)*

11 *Addresses*

BEARR Trust (British Emergency Action in Russia and the Republics)
Chichester House
278 High Holborn
London WC1V 7ER
Tel: 0171-404 7081
Fax: 0171-404 7103

CEDAG (European Council for Voluntary Organisations)
18 rue de Varenne
F-75007 Paris
France
Tel: 00 33 1 45 49 06 58
Fax: 00 33 1 42 84 04 84

Charity Know How
114-118 Southampton Row
London WC1B 5AA
Tel: 0171-831 7798
Fax: 0171-831 0134

COFACE (Confederation of Family Organisations)
rue de Londres, 17
B-1050 Brussels
Belgium
Tel: 00 32 2 511 41 79
Fax: 00 32 2 514 47 73

Community Development Foundation
60 Highbury Grove
London N5 2AG
Tel: 0171-226 5375
Fax: 0171-704 0313

Directory of Social Change
Radius Works
Back Lane
London NW3 1HL
Tel: 0171-435 8171
Fax: 0171-794 7724

ECAS (Euro-Citizen-Action-Service)
rue Defacqz, 1
B-1050 Brussels
Belgium
Tel: 00 32 2 534 51 66
Fax: 00 32 2 534 52 75

European Anti-Poverty Network
205 rue Bélliard, Bte 13
B-1040 Brussels
Belgium
Tel: 00 32 2 230 44 55
Fax: 00 32 2 230 97 33

European Foundation Centre
51 rue de la Concorde
B-1050 Brussels
Belgium
Tel: 00 32 2 512 89 38
Fax: 00 32 2 512 32 65

ICOM (Industrial Common Ownership Movement)
Vassalli House
20 Central Road
Leeds LS1 6DE
Tel: 0113-246 1737
Fax: 0113-244 0002

Local Government International Bureau
35 Great Smith Street
London SW1P 3BJ
Tel: 0171-222 1636
Fax: 0171-233 2179

Nigel Tarling (Euro/International Officer)
National Council for Voluntary Organisations
Regent's Wharf
8 All Saints Street
London N1 9RL
Tel: 0171-713 6161
Fax: 0171-713 6300
Minicom: 0171-278 1289

12 Bibliography

Publications by:

Directory of Social Change

Derek Allen, *Tax and Giving in Europe 1993/4*, DSC, 3rd edition, 1993

Brian Dabson (ed), *Company Giving in Europe*, DSC, 1st edition, 1991

John Griffiths, *Promoting Corporate Community Investment in Europe*, DSC for CCIE, 1st edition, 1993

Karina Holly (ed), *Associations and Foundations in the EC – Legal, Structural and Fiscal Issues*, DSC with NCVO and ECAS

Ruth Lauer and Steve England (eds), *US Foundation Support in Europe*, DSC, 2nd edition, 1994

David Logan, *A Guide to Transnational Giving*, DSC, 1st edition, 1993

Richard Macfarlane and Jean-Louis Laville, *Developing Community Partnerships in Europe*, DSC, 1st edition, 1993

Euro-Citizen-Action-Service

A Guide to EC Funding for NGOs, the EC's Most Colourful Flowers. A guide to the main sources of EC funding (known as 'budget lines'), published in October 1993.

National Council for Voluntary Organisations

John Bennington, Jill Russell and Sean Baine, *Changing Europe: Challenges Facing the Voluntary and Community Sectors in the 1990s*, NCVO Publications and Community Development Foundation, 1992

Ann Davison, *Grants from Europe: How to Get Money and Influence Policy*, NCVO Publications, 7th edition, 1993

Brian Harvey, *Networking in Europe: A Guide to European Voluntary Organisations*, NCVO Publications and Community Development Foundation, 1994 (2nd edition available March 1995)

Maggie MacDonald and Ute Kowarzik, *Developing Transnational Partnerships: A Guide for Voluntary Organisations Working on EC-Funded Projects*, NCVO Publications, 1993